YORK'S MILITARY LEGACY

IAN D. ROTHERHAM

Pen & Sword
MILITARY

In memory of the many soldiers and others from York who suffered or gave their lives in numerous conflicts over the centuries. Most remain unnamed and unknown, but the seven First World War VC heroes are Lieutenant Colonel Bertram Best-Dunkley, Corporal Harry Blanshard Wood, Private Arthur Poulter, Lieutenant Donald Bell, Captain Archie White, Private Tom Dresser and Private Charles Hull.

First published in Great Britain in 2017 by
PEN AND SWORD MILITARY
an imprint of
Pen and Sword Books Ltd
47 Church Street
Barnsley
South Yorkshire S70 2AS

ISBN 978 1 52670 925 7

The right of Ian D. Rotherham to be identified as the author of this work
has been asserted in accordance with the Copyright, Designs and Patents Act 1988.

Every reasonable effort has been made to trace copyright holders of material reproduced in this book,
but if any have been inadvertently overlooked the publishers will be pleased to hear from them.

Typeset by Aura Technology and Software Services, India
Printed and bound in Malta by Gutenberg

Pen & Sword Books Ltd incorporates the imprints of Pen & Sword
Archaeology, Atlas, Aviation, Battleground, Discovery, Family History, History, Maritime, Military,
Naval, Politics, Railways, Select, Social History, Transport, True Crime, Claymore Press, Frontline
Books, Leo Cooper, Praetorian Press, Remember When, Seaforth Publishing and Wharncliffe.

For a complete list of Pen and Sword titles please contact
Pen and Sword Books Limited
47 Church Street, Barnsley, South Yorkshire, S70 2AS, England
email: enquiries@pen-and-sword.co.uk
website: www.pen-and-sword.co.uk

CONTENTS

Chronology   4

1. Introduction   11

2. Early History   16

3. Local Conflict up to the Norman Conquest   25

4. Harrying of the North   38

5. Post-Conquest York & England at War   46

6. The English Civil War   65

7. The Jacobite Rebellion   74

8. The Second World War & The Cold War   87

9. Service, Honours & Awards   96

10. The Military Heritage   102

11. The Walls & Other Defences   112

Selected Bibliography   127

Acknowledgements   128

About the author   128

CHRONOLOGY

71 AD: Roman general Quintus Cerialis establishes York by building a fortress on land between the rivers Foss and Ouse.

78 AD: Roman general Agricola (Gnaeus Julius Agricola), having become governor of Britain in AD 77, uses York as one of his forward bases from which to subdue Scotland. He maintains or establishes important routes from the south via Castleford on dry ground to the west and via Brough on low-lying ground subject to flood risk, in the east.

117 AD: Last records of the so-called 'Lost Ninth' legion.

120 AD: Emperor Hadrian is based in York and is responsible for initiating the great stone-built wall across northern England to separate it from the land of the Picts.

122 AD: Hadrian has a shrine built in York to the goddess Britannia, with coins struck with a female figure as the personification of Britain.

200 AD: Late in his reign, Emperor Septimus Severus travels to Britain and sets about work to strengthen Hadrian's Wall and to reoccupy the more northerly Antonine Wall, and in 208 AD, he sets about an invasion of Caledonia (i.e. today's Scotland). He also makes York a *colonia* with special powers. However, the invasion ends prematurely when he is taken ill in late 210 AD and dies at Eboracum, i.e. York, in 211 AD.

305 AD: In the midst of a long period of political and military intrigue and vying for imperial power, Constantine (Flavius Valerius Aurelius Constantinus Augustus) arrives in Britain with his father, Caesar (i.e. Deputy Emperor in the West), Constantius. They spend a year based out of York and at war with the Picts. However, while in York in July 306 AD, Constantius dies. Constantine II or the Great is declared Emperor of Rome by the army based at Eboracum. Constantine is a hugely influential figure in history becoming the first Roman Emperor to convert to Christianity.

350 AD: During the fourth century AD, York's success is on the wane, with its economy in decline and its population shrinking. Increasingly threatened by barbarian incursions, new work is undertaken on digging defensive ditches and a new tower, the Anglian Tower, constructed.

400 AD: Rome abandons Britain to address issues back in Italy.

500 AD: The Saxons now settling across the area give the former city the name of Eoforwīc or Eoforīc, in Old English meaning the 'wild boar town' or land 'with plentiful wild boar'; and the modern name of York emerges.

600 AD: York is by now once more a significant centre, power base and trading port known as Eoforwic. This is an important royal centre for Northumbrian Saxon kings, King Edwin of Northumbria being baptized here in 627 AD.

625 AD: Paulinus of York (later St Paulinus) (died 10th October 644) is a Roman missionary and the first Bishop of York. He chooses York to establish a timber church, as the forerunner of York Minster.

866 AD: York falls to the Viking invaders, first captured in November by Ivar the Boneless. He leads a substantial army of Danish Vikings, called by Anglo-Saxon chroniclers, the Great Heathen Army. They had landed in East Anglia where King Edmund bought them off with a supply of horses before they headed north to York.

867 AD: Rival Saxon contenders for the Northumbrian crown join forces to retake York from the Danes but fail in the attempt.

875 AD: York's importance as the centre of power in Northumbria is strengthened as Viking Halfdan Ragnarsson seizes power.

927 AD: Saxon King Athelstan, grandson of Alfred the Great, takes control of York from Viking King Gofraid ua Ímair.

937 AD: The major Saxon victory at the Battle of Brunanburh to unite England under Saxon rule.

946 & 952 AD: Viking Eric Bloodaxe has two reigns as the last king of York or Jorvic.

1066 AD: On 20th September the Battle of Fulford is fought on the outskirts of the village of Fulford with a Viking force led by Harald Hardrada and Tostig Godwinson inflicting a significant defeat on the Northumbrian Saxon earls Edwin and Morcar. York is spared from sacking.

1066 AD: On 25th September the Battle of Stamford Bridge is fought between the Saxon army under King Harold Godwinson and the invading Viking force of King Harald Hardrada of Norway and Harold's brother Tostig; both the latter die and the Viking force is annihilated.

1066 AD: On 14th October Harold's Saxon army is heavily defeated at the Battle of Hastings and Harold II is killed; the Norman Conquest is underway and York is to suffer.

1068: York Castle is built as a wooden structure with a typical motte and bailey.

1069: The brutal 'Harrying of the North' with punitive genocide by the Normans against the northern Saxons.

1069: York Castle is burnt down and rebuilt in stone during the following years.

1088: Norman earl Alan Rufus becomes very successful and powerful in northern England; as a patron of York he founds St Mary's Abbey.

1138: On 22nd August on Cowton Moor, the Battle of the Standard takes place near Northallerton in North Yorkshire as English forces of King Stephen repel the Scottish army. Preaching that to battle the Scots was to do God's work York's Archbishop Thurstan helped raise the army.

1190: What was to become Clifford's Tower, part of the castle, is the site of the burning to death of several hundred Jews.

1200s: York city walls are rebuilt in stone to protect the city from marauding Scots.

1319: A violent and troublesome period during the reigns of Edward I – the 'Hammer of the Scots' – and Edward II with raids south toward York by the Scots. A major invasion by Malcolm of Scotland fails to take York; unable to enter the city and capture Queen Isabella, the army turns back.

1322: The Battle of Boroughbridge is fought on 16th March between rebellious barons led by the king's cousin, Thomas Earl of Lancaster, and King Edward II of England.

1322: The Battle of Old Byland is a significant conflict in October between English and Scottish troops and is a catastrophic defeat for the English.

1322: For rebelling against Edward II, Roger de Clifford is hanged alive in chains from what then became known as Clifford's Tower.

1455–85: The War of the Cousins later known as the Wars of the Roses.

1460: In October, the Act of Accord names Richard Duke of York as King of England taking the succession away from Henry's six-year-old son.

1460: 30th December defeat of Richard II at the Battle of Wakefield; Edward Duke of York claims the throne as King Edward IV.

1460: The heads of the Duke of York, the Duke of Rutland, and the earl of Salisbury are displayed on spikes on Micklegate Bar.

1461: The Battle of Ferrybridge takes place on 28th March as a build-up to the bloody Battle of Towton.

1461: The Battle of Towton is fought on 29th March south-east of York and is one of the most violent conflicts ever on English soil.

1461: King Edward IV of the House of York begins his rule.

1483: Edward IV dies and his brother Richard Duke of York becomes King Richard III.

1483: Richard dies on 22nd August at the Battle of Bosworth.

1536: The Pilgrimage of Grace protests to King Henry VIII, asking for religious tolerance. Robert Aske occupies York with around 9,000 protestors.

1537: After a further uprising, the protestors are defeated and the leaders hanged.

1642–51: The English Civil War and a further period of turmoil for royalist York.

1643: The Siege of York is relieved by Prince Rupert on 28th June and the Parliamentarians withdraw on 1st July.

1644: The Battle of Marston Moor is fought on 2nd July 1644 with a first defeat for the royalist commander Prince Rupert; this crushing defeat for the Royalists leads to the renewal of the siege, and ultimately the surrender of York on July 15th to the Roundheads.

1644: In July, following defeat by the Parliamentary forces, there is considerable pillaging and looting with important buildings destroyed. Further destruction is limited only by the personal intervention of Lord Fairfax, a Yorkshireman, to save York's churches, especially the Minster.

1660: York recovers from the impact of the war to become the third-largest city in England following London and Norwich.

1685: The first of the Yorkshire regiments is established. James Stuart, Duke of York, becomes King James II.

1715: The first Jacobite uprising.

1745: The second Jacobite uprising.

1745: Archbishop of York, Thomas Herring is described as 'the last warrior bishop of England'.

1746: By January, York has raised and armed a substantial militia force against the Jacobites.

1746: The Duke of Cumberland (known in Scotland as 'The Butcher') defeats the Jacobites at Culloden near Inverness and is presented with the freedom of the city of York in a hundred-guinea gold box.

1746: Twenty-two Jacobite rebels are executed at York.

1745–54: Two heads from executed rebels are placed on Micklegate Bar and remain there until stolen in 1754.

1757: The last defensive use of the walls when taxation protestors rioted.

1759: At the Battle of Minden on 1st August Yorkshiremen of the 51st Regiment (predecessor of the King's Own Yorkshire Light Infantry) pick white roses from bushes close to the battlefield as a tribute to their fallen comrades.

1797: Fulford cavalry barracks opened.

1700s & 1800s: York-based battalions are involved in major conflicts in Europe and then around the world.

1877–78: Fulford is rebuilt as infantry barracks.

1800s & 1900s: York is involved as a training location with military barracks and camps.

1800s: Demolition of stretches of walls and gates triggers protests for their repair and retention.

1884: Strensall Camp is established for training combat troops by the War Office on around 1,800 acres of land.

1914–19: York-based battalions involved in many major battles and conflicts.

1929: York Castle, long since converted into a civilian prison, finally closes its custodial function as a military detention centre.

1930s–45: York and its environs become strategically important for the development of RAF bomber command airfields and the training of pilots and crews for the attacks on Europe.

1942: On 29th April, York suffers retaliatory bombing as part of the so-called 'Baedeker Blitz' by the German Luftwaffe resulting in ninety-two deaths, hundreds of injuries, and destruction or damage to historic buildings.

1950s: Fulford Barracks is renamed Imphal Barracks in honour of the role of the West Yorkshire Regiment at the Second World War Battle of Imphal, Manipur, India.

1950s & 1960s: York is the base for a Cold War bunker built in 1961 to monitor impacts of potential nuclear attack.

1974: On 11th June, the Provisional Irish Republican Army plants and detonates bombs at Strensall Camp.

1991: The secret bunker is closed

2006: The secret bunker opens as a museum and Listed Building.

2006: The Yorkshire Regiment is formed from three major existing regiments.

2013: Duncombe Barracks is notified of impending closure.

2021: The closure will end nearly 150 years of military usage of Strensall Common.

2030: The planned closure of last combat-related function at York.

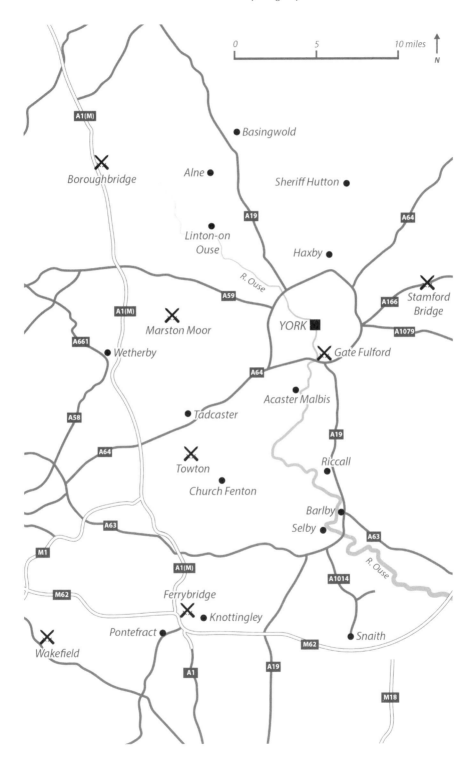

1. INTRODUCTION

Fought near to or around York, Towton, Stamford Bridge, Marston Moor and Fulford were some of the most infamous and bloodiest battles fought on English soil. It is said that Yorkshire has had more major skirmishes than any other English county. Lesser-known battles include Sherburn-in-Elmet where Parliamentarians defeated the last significant Royalist force in the north of England. Because of its location, York has long been significant, both politically and militarily. For centuries the north of England was vulnerable to local strife and, potentially more serious, to raids south from Scotland. This was a problem before the Romans and continued into the Middle Ages; any hint of trouble or weakness south of the border would tempt the Scots to raid.

One of the oldest settlements in Western Europe, York has changed and been changed by waves of settlers and conquerors. The reason for its origins and longevity is its location on the River Ouse at the River Foss confluence, and close to the rivers Derwent and Wharfe. Historically navigable from the great Humber Estuary but surrounded by Yorkshire fens, York could be reached relatively easily by early settlers; and communication or trade to the coast and across the North Sea to Europe was possible. With overland transportation difficult or impossible, this route inland from the coast to York provided penetration deep into the northern English countryside.

A view of the city of York from the River Ouse from the *Modern Universal British Traveller* in the late 1700s to show the town and the river transport.

York grew and developed on dry land with protective rivers and associated wet-lands giving security and mobility. Early, prehistoric settlement was on nearby drier, raised areas along the floodplain. Here the Romans settled to build a great, north-ern, fortified city and military settlement from which they could foray overland into northern England or by ship and the coastal route to Scotland and the Picts. York's significance was emphasized when Constantine was made Emperor while residing there.

Following lean times after Roman abandonment and Saxon neglect, when the Vikings swept into northern England York was much to their liking, thus Jorvic was reborn as their capital city. Once subsumed into Anglo-Saxon Northumbria, York continued its huge strategic and military significance through late Saxon times, during the Norman Conquest, and into medieval England. Indeed, two of the most far-reaching battles in English history were fought at nearby Fulford and Stamford Bridge. York's military significance grew again during the Wars of the Roses, with the Battle Towton in 1461 described as the most barbaric ever fought on British soil.

Following oscillating and vicious disputes over religion during the reigns of the later Tudors, divisive and punitive civil war played out again under the Stuart kings and Parliamentary Commonwealth. Through all this, York was a major strategic location in northern England, an important base for those commanding it and a significant prize for those who did not. This military importance declined into modern times but the city retains garrison and regimental ties. The last direct conflict occurred when York was targeted for retaliatory Baedeker Blitz by German bombers during April 1942.

York Castle by F. Place, about 1699.

York's remarkable history and longevity, and its significance in English and sometimes international politics and economics, have left a unique, unparalleled military history. Some key points:

1. York holds a strategic location between the rivers and on dry land surrounded by extensive wetlands
2. The city's origins were as a Roman legionary centre in the north of England
3. As Jorvic it became the Viking capital of northern England
4. Twice, York was a civil war stronghold and disputed territory
5. Up to the present day, the city is home to modern regiments
6. As one of the *Baedeker Guide* cities, York was a target of Hitler's retaliatory blitz

There are various reasons for the city's amazingly long timeline of military history and significance. Interestingly today for reasons of the strategic development of modern warfare and conflict, this remarkable role is drawing to a close in the early twenty-first century. It leaves a legacy of heritage and a rich, associated tourism economy. York's importance has been for one major reason: location, location, location. The River Ouse via the massive Humber Estuary provided access to the very heart of northern England when overland travel was problematic. For invaders this provided a good route in, but also a quick exit if things turned bad.

York Minster from the River Ouse, around 1800.

Left: Military Sunday parade, 1907.

Below: Haxby Road Military Hospital in about 1917.

ARMS OF THE CITY OF YORK

ARMS OF THE SEE OF YORK

Above left: The City of York coat of arms.

Above right: The coat of arms of the See of York.

York was a key controlling point for the Kingdom of Northumbria, for the north of England, and a buffer to Scottish incursions too. Furthermore, the city was situated far enough north for a London-based monarch to wield power in the North, but not too far to be a problem in returning south to London or else the midlands such as Nottingham. In the later days of its significance, such as the Second World War, York's location and topography were key with extensive flatlands in eastern England, ideal for launching bombing raids over Nazi Germany. From the Romans to the Cold War, York has a rich military heritage.

2. EARLY HISTORY

York is known throughout the world because of its historic association with famous moments in English history, from Roman stronghold, to Viking capital. However, the lifeblood of this remarkable city is the great River Ouse which runs north to south through York and then across the south-eastern lowlands of the Vale of York before, joined to the River Derwent, discharging to the massive Humber Estuary and thus the North Sea. This strategic location has been the cause both of York's military importance and of its growth to become a city; in short its contribution to British history. Gordon Home, in *Yorkshire*, published in 1908 summarizes this nicely:

> Thoroughly to master the story of the city of York is to know practically the whole of English history. Its importance from the earliest times has made York the centre of all the chief events that have taken place in the North of England; and right up to the time of the Civil War the great happenings of the country always affected York, and brought the northern capital into the vortex of affairs. And yet, despite the prominent part the city has played in ecclesiastical, military, and civil affairs through so many centuries of strife, it has contrived to retain a medieval character in many ways unequalled by any town in the kingdom.

Though now a large, increasingly sprawling city, old York itself is on slightly raised ground above the great floodplain dominated by the River Ouse. While modern urbanization has changed much of the old city, enough remains to give a genuine feel of the remarkable past, York having an historic core far more intact than most towns and cities. As a city, York originated in the early first millennium AD though there is archaeological evidence of people in the area back as far as around 8,000 BC. Indeed, finds of polished stone axes

A Roman coffin at York.

A Roman general
depicted at the time of
Constantine.

evidence people during Neolithic times. There was early settlement on the south-west bank of the River Ouse, near the modern-day Scarborough Bridge. Later flint tools and weapons close to Holgate Beck and the River Ouse show Bronze Age occupation. On the south-west bank of the Ouse are Iron Age burial sites with farming settlement and by Roman times, York emerged as a major town; the Celtic name of Eboracum or Eburacum is known from Roman sources. This archaeology suggests that from early times this was a favoured place for people to settle, live, and ultimately, defend. Location between rivers and wetlands provided natural defence and yet being 'on' a major river gave easy access in and out if needed or for trade. The downside, as York knows to its cost, is a propensity to flood.

From the Romano-British period York's military and political significance grew. The Romans called the local Celtic tribes the Brigantes and the Parisii, and York was probably sited on the border between the two. During the Roman invasion and conquest of Britain, the Brigantes became a Roman 'client state'. However, as their leaders became more hostile to Rome, to subdue possible unrest, the Roman general Quintus Petillius Cerialis led the Ninth Legion northward through England and north of the Humber. The move is significant in this military timeline and in the history of the city, York being founded in 71 AD when Quintus Cerialis constructed a military fortress (or *castra*) on flat ground above the floodland of the River Ouse. The location was close to the confluence with the lesser river, the Foss.

The fortress to house around 6,000 troops was later rebuilt in stone, and grew to cover around 25 hectares. We find the earliest note of 'Eburacum' on a wooden stylus tablet from about 100 AD from the Roman fortress of Vindolanda near Hadrian's Wall; clearly soldiers from York went northward to guard the frontier. Nowadays, much of the Roman fort lies beneath York Minster's foundations but some original walls remain. Over history

The Constantine Triumphal Arch in Rome.

Alexanders brought to England by the Romans

Evidence of the military history of York can be found in certain wild flowers in and around the city. Some of these came back from the Mediterranean and the Middle East with the Crusaders or with monastic orders, and some may have arrived with the Romans. A great variety of wild flowers is found around the outer sides of the city wall ramparts, and near Micklegate Bar is a good place for this. Described as 'the most historically intriguing plant of the ramparts', the wild alexanders or 'parsley of Alexandria', may have been brought to Britain by the Romans. This distinctive, tall, Mediterranean flower with its bright yellow blooms was first recorded here under the city walls in the 1780s. The plant was important as a spring vegetable and for its herbal-medical properties, being a general tonic. The whole of the plant is edible with metre-high, celery-like stems, glossy, dark-green leaves, and black seeds. Interestingly, even today this flower is uncommon inland and the idea of its arrival in York with the Roman legions is nice if a little fanciful.

however, as with many sites, Roman stones and bricks were robbed and re-used for later building. Roman military sites came with sophisticated bathing and recreational facilities and York was no exception. The site of the Roman baths was refound in 1930 under a tavern in St Sampson's Square, the remains now open to public viewing via the appropriately named Roman Bath public house.

In about 120 AD, the Sixth Legion replaced the Ninth Legion at York, but there is no record of the Ninth after 117 AD, the so-called 'Lost Legion'. There have been various suggestions regarding the fate of the 'lost' Ninth and these include annihilation by the Picts in Scotland to a strategic military move to the Mediterranean. The mystery has become the stuff of legend. However, the presence of the Sixth Legion was more long-lived and they remained in York until the Roman withdrawal around 400 AD. At this time, pressure along the pagan borders of the Empire, meant legions being recalled to Rome.

With the Roman establishment of York, the city acquired political and military significance that lasted for much of the subsequent two thousand years. The Roman emperors Hadrian, Septimius Severus and Constantius I all chose York as their base during campaigns in northern England and northward into Scotland. Indeed, it was while staying at York that Emperor Severus made York the capital of Britannia Inferior, and granted it the privileges of a *colonia* or city, one of only four in Britain. Most famously perhaps, when Constantius I died in York, the troops based here proclaimed his son, Constantine the Great, as Emperor of Rome.

Having substantial military, political and administrative roles, York rapidly grew in economic importance. The workshops necessary to supply the needs of 5,000 or more troops garrisoned there included a military pottery, tile kilns, glass-working at Coppergate, metalworks, and leatherworks for the legion situated in Tanner Row. By 237 AD, the York

Constantine the Great

Flavius Valerius Aurelius Constantinus Augustus *c.* 272 AD – 22 May 337 AD, also known as Constantine I or Saint Constantine, was Emperor of Rome from 306 AD to 337 AD. He was the son of Flavius Valerius Constantius, a senior Roman army officer, and his consort Helena, and who, in 293 AD, was made Caesar, or Deputy Emperor, in the West.

The young Constantine was sent east and rose through the ranks, becoming a military tribune under emperors Diocletian and Galerius. In 305 AD, with Constantius made Augustus, and thus senior Western Emperor, Constantine was sent west to join his father's British campaigns. Then, after the death of Constantius in York in 306 AD, Constantine was declared emperor and by 324 AD, following civil wars against the opposition emperors Maxentius and Licinius, he became ruler of both west and east.

Constantine acquired a reputation as a strong and capable ruler and military leader and undertook or initiated reforms of administrative, financial, social, and military procedures to make the empire more robust and more effective. His reforms included the Roman army reorganized as mobile field units with garrison soldiers to deal with both internal problems and incursions by tribes of barbarians. Government was restructured and the authorities for civil and military matters were separated. His innovations included the striking of a new gold coin, called the *solidus*, and this became standard for Byzantine and European currencies for nearly a millennium.

One of Constantine's great claims to fame and to subsequent historic influence was his conversion to Christianity. He was influential in the Edict of Milan in 313 AD, to provide religious tolerance for Christianity across the Roman Empire, and in 325 AD initiated the First Council of Nicaea.

Constantine's military campaigns were well away from York where he had been declared emperor. They included wars with tribes along the Roman frontiers such as the Franks, the Alamanni, the Goths, and the Sarmatians. Constantine's rule is considered to be a distinctive and important period in the history of the Roman Empire: he commissioned a new imperial residence at Byzantium which was renamed Constantinople in his own honour. The city later became the capital of the Empire for over a thousand years.

His reputation grew throughout the lifetime of his children well after his own reign. The medieval church presented Constantine as a paragon of virtue and civil leaders took him as a model for imperial legitimacy and governance. However, there was more critical analysis of his period in office from the Renaissance onward. Sources were discovered which described him as a tyrant and oppressive. Nevertheless, Constantine was a hugely significant figure in the history of Christianity and hence of Europe. On his personal orders the Church of the Holy Sepulchre in Jerusalem was constructed at the supposed site of Jesus's tomb and was to become the holiest place in Christendom. Furthermore, his influence on Papal status was considerable and by Eastern Orthodox, Byzantine Catholic, and Anglican churches he is venerated as a saint. The significance for our story here is that his rise to success began in the heart of York.

Emperor Constantine's victory at the Battle of Miliran Bridge.

Roman altars at York.

colonia was a thriving centre with trade based around the military centre encouraging local people to establish a permanent settlement close by on the south-west bank of the Ouse opposite the fortress.

Such *coloniae* were in part established to benefit retired soldiers, and this meant York was self-governing, with a council of wealthy civilians (including merchants), and military veterans. When around 400 AD York's fortunes took a downturn with the withdrawal of Roman imperial support; the situation became increasingly intolerable. Bad weather combined with the location chosen for defence and river access led to increasing problems. Set between two flood-prone rivers, York suffered periodic winter inundations and no longer maintained the riverside wharfs (important for trade) that silted up. The main Roman bridge over the River Ouse decayed and became unusable, and while Eboracum was still an administrative centre, the associated civilian town largely disappeared. The *colonia* area was mostly above the flood levels but over time this was abandoned as York was reduced to a small population only on a narrow strip of dry ground.

In the post-Roman period, Anglo-Saxon colonists arrived in Britain. First of all they were employed as military mercenaries to protect the post-Roman British population from invasion, but this strategy soon caused major problems. When they liked what they found they decided to stay and thus displaced the indigenous local communities. For York, the modern name of York emerged as the Old English Eoforwīc or Eoforīc, which means the 'wild boar town' or land 'with plentiful wild boar', and later Norse settlers adopted the name Jórvík.

As Anglo-Saxons settled across northern England, York grew again, as the Anglian regional and later Northumbrian capital. Indeed, by the early seventh century, York was again an important royal centre, but this was now for the Northumbrian Saxon kings. Paulinus of York (later St Paulinus) chose York to establish a timber church, the forerunner of York Minster, and King Edwin of Northumbria was baptized here in 627 AD.

Engraved for Sydney's History of England.

Wale delin.   Walker sculp.

PAULINUS baptizing EDWIN,
the first Christian King of Northumberland, at York.

Paulinus at York baptizing Edwin as the first Christian king of Northumbria.

Roman fortifications showing wall and multi-angular tower, Museum Gardens, York. (Photo Kaly99)

The first Minster was probably built about this time although since timber structures frequently leave only sparse remains, it is unclear exactly where.

Over subsequent centuries, York developed as an important centre for royal and ecclesiastical affairs. There was the appointment firstly of a bishop, and then, from 735 AD, an archbishop. With Saxon buildings mostly of timber not stone, and only limited written records, there is little known of the city during this period. However, with Northumbrian rule, York grew as a centre of learning, acquiring a library and a Minster school. A hugely significant pupil of the school was a man called Alcuin who became its master and then adviser to Emperor Charlemagne. Frustratingly, we have little detail of this important place in the kingdom of Northumbria or in the growth of Christian learning. Archaeological research indicates the walls of the Roman fortress survived reasonably intact with the 'Anglian Tower' filling a gap in the Roman Way, perhaps a repair during the Anglian period. Since the walls and gates survived, the layout of the Roman streets was also intact within the old fortress and the great hall, the Roman legionary building, was used until the ninth century.

By the eighth century, York was once again a thriving commercial settlement having trade links across England, and via its river and the Humber, across the North Sea to Europe. The latter were particularly with northern France, the Low Countries and Rhineland. The remains of buildings from the seventh and ninth centuries have been found near the Foss and Ouse confluence and may indicate a trading settlement for nearby royal and ecclesiastical centres.

3. LOCAL CONFLICT UP TO THE NORMAN CONQUEST

The Romans

The Roman influence and military significance of York have already been noted, and upstanding remains have inspired writers down the centuries; for example, Gordon Home in *Yorkshire*: 'Of the Roman legionary base called Eboracum there still remain parts of the wall and the lower portion of a thirteen-sided angle bastion, while embedded in the medieval earthen ramparts there is a great deal of Roman walling.'

Britons, Saxons & Vikings

Saxon settlement followed the Roman retreat, and then, especially across eastern and northern England, Norse tribes raided and then invaded. This history was introduced in

The last Viking king of York, the infamous Eric Bloodaxe.

the previous chapter. In 866 AD however, there came a new wave of aggressive colonizers, York being captured by Viking invaders led by Ivar the Boneless with a large army of Danes, (known to later Anglo-Saxon writers as the Great Heathen Army). After landing in East Anglia they headed northward to take the prize city of York. However, by 867 AD, squabbling rival Saxon contenders for the Northumbrian crown forged an alliance to try and recapture the city but failed and their leaders were killed.

The Archbishop of York, the Saxon Wulfhere, appeared to have collaborated with the Vikings but was expelled from York when a Northumbrian uprising in 872 AD was only in part successful. Wulfhere returned to York and remained as Archbishop until his death, and significantly the Viking, King Guthred, was buried in York Minster. This suggests he converted to Christianity presumably under the influence of Wulfhere.

Across the region, Viking coins from this period all seem to be from the York mint, again suggesting the city's importance in the Viking-influenced kingdom of Northumbria. York's importance as the seat of Northumbria was further confirmed when the Scandinavian warlord, Guthrum, headed for East Anglia, and another Viking, Halfdan Ragnarsson seized power in 875 AD.

However, the city achieved particular notoriety with the arrival of Eric Bloodaxe, the last king based at York. Eric Haraldsson (c. 885–954 AD), nicknamed 'Eric Bloodaxe', was a tenth-century Norwegian ruler, believed to have had short, violent periods as king of Norway, king of Orkney, and twice as king of Northumbria (c. 947–948 AD, 952–954 AD). Eric's reigns are mysterious and controversial since historical sources are rather vague. At heart a pagan, Eric perhaps converted to Christianity when crowned king at York, and subsequently died in battle or was perhaps murdered.

Eric's life and reign remain shrouded in uncertainty, but as king of Northumbria of that there is some historical detail. Sources such as the *Anglo-Saxon Chronicle*, *Historia Regum* and Roger of Wendover's *Historia Anglorum* are rather vague and the chronologies appear muddled. The ancient kingdom of Northumbria was subject to bitter conflict between West Saxon kings and Vikings, particularly the Hiberno-Norse descendants of Ímair, king of Dublin from 873 to 881 AD. However, the roles and allegiances of the Northumbrians were always somewhat fluid, giving rise to an assessment by later historians that they were undependable.

In 927 AD, the Saxon King Athelstan, grandson of Alfred the Great took control of York from Gofraid ua Ímair. This act was followed by major victory at the Battle of Brunanburh in 937 AD, which according to some authorities was probably fought along a major cross-kingdom boundary from modern-day east Sheffield and across South Yorkshire. The location of the battle-site has long-been debated but could well have been around the Tinsley gap east of Sheffield and maybe through to Barnburgh in the Dearne Valley. Lands in the area were later governed by Saxon nobleman Wulfric Spott, and it is suggested his role was in part to keep order in the contested borderlands between Northumbria and Mercia.

In the earlier part of the 900s, Athelstan and his half-brother Edmund defeated Gofraid's son King Olaf Guthfrithson of Dublin, plus Northumbrians, Welsh and Scottish kings and princes. This battle with the catastrophic slaughter of royalty and nobility on both sides consolidated Athelstan's power. Decisive victory brought Northumbria and York within the wider fold of England together with Wessex and Mercia. Royal charters issued from 937 to 939 AD, toward the end of Athelstan's reign note the king as 'ruler over all Britain' (*totius rex Brittanniae*); York was as so often the case, a focus for those seeking control and for those wishing to usurp authority.

For York however, this stability was not long-lasting and when Athelstan died in 939 AD his successor, 18-year-old Edmund, was unable to retain control of Northumbria. Already by 940 AD, as Edmund came to power, the new head of the Uí Ímair dynasty had based his activities and power in York. The *Irish Annals* suggest that Olaf Guthfrithson had departed Dublin in 939 AD and in 940 was joined in York by his cousin, Amlaíb Cuarán or known in England as Olaf Sihtricsson. Olaf Guthfrithson died in 941 AD and was succeeded by Sihtricsson, the *Anglo-Saxon Chronicle* stating this was with popular local support: 'The Northumbrians belied their pledges, and chose Olaf from Ireland as their king.' Sihtricsson reigned jointly with his nephew Ragnald (Rögnvaldr), son of Gofraid. The history is full of intrigue and it was suggested that Wulfstan, Archbishop of York and one of the leading Northumbrian statesmen, was central to this popular acceptance. As so often the case in Northumbria, he later switched his allegiance.

However, by 942 AD, Edmund recaptured Mercia and the Five Boroughs of Danelaw but in retaliation, Olaf hit back with a successful raid on Tamworth in the heart of Mercia and former capital city. Edmund laid siege to Olaf and his army at Leicester, a Danelaw borough, and the Vikings barely escaped; negotiations followed leading to short-lived peace. Edmund accepted Olaf as his ally and ceded to him Northumbria south to Watling Street. This was followed by Olaf's conversion to Christianity with Edmund as sponsor for his baptism and then the same for Ragnall's confirmation. Nevertheless, despite the show of friendship, by 944 AD, Edmund drove out both Viking rulers and Northumbria passed once more into West Saxon control. The chroniclers said Archbishop Wulfstan and the ealdorman of the Mercians deposed the 'deserters', most likely 'born-again pagans', forcing them to accept Edmund as king. That same year, King Edmund attacked the independent kingdom of Cumbria to place it under the control King Malcolm I of Scotland. This was in exchange for Malcolm's support 'both on sea and on land', which would be a useful allegiance against the Irish Norse. By 945 AD, Olaf Sihtricsson returned to Dublin and Ragnald died, and Edmund was described in one of his charters as '*rex totiusque Albionis primicerius*'. However, he was killed in 946 AD, apparently assassinated on 26th May, by Leofa, an exiled thief. This was while the king attended St Augustine's Day mass in Pucklechurch, South Gloucestershire. It was suggested this may have been political in-fighting, with Edmund succeeded by his brother Eadred who reigned from 946 until 955 AD.

With both Northumbrian and Scottish loyalties unstable and unreliable, Eadred brought the North under his control, chronicles recording that he 'reduced all the land of Northumbria to his control; and the Scots granted him oaths that they would do all that he wanted'. This was followed by the convening of the Northumbrian witan with Archbishop Wulfstan at Tanshelf (modern-day Pontefract, in West Yorkshire), in 947 AD.

At this site near the River Aire, by the old Roman road on what was known as the Roman Ridge, they pledged obedience to him as their king. Neither in Northumbria nor York was English rule welcomed.

In typical fashion, the Northumbrians ignored their recent pledges and oaths so that by 948 AD, 'they had taken Eric for their king'. By way of a response, King Eadred marched his forces northward with a violent raid into Northumbria, including the burning of Ripon Minster which had been founded by St Wilfrid in 672 AD. Despite suffering heavy casualties at the Battle of Castleford *(Ceaster forda)*, near Tanshelf, Eadred's raid was regarded as successful and as they returned southward, the Northumbrians decided to appease the English king. They renounced Eric and paid Eadred compensation, the clear message being that if they persisted in their independence from the southern Anglo-Saxons, the consequences would be severe.

However, for the Northumbrians they faced problems from both south and from north, the Scots. The *Chronicle of the Kings of Alba* noted that in '948 or 949, Malcolm I of Scotland and Cumbria raided Northumbria as far south as the River Tees and returned with many cattle and captives'. This may have been a military strike in favour of Eric. However, in the absence of Eric, the Irish Vikings once again laid claim to York and Anlaf Cwiran (or Olaf) having been defeated at Slane in what is now County Meath in Ireland, in 947 AD returned to Northumbria and assumed the kingship, supposedly in 949. Eadred seemed to turn a blind eye to this move by his brother's godson. Nevertheless in 952 AD it was stated that, 'the Northumbrians drove out King Olaf and accepted Eric, son of Harold'. Also in 952 AD, *The Annals of Ulster* noted a victory of the 'foreigners' (Northmen or the Norse-Gaels) over 'the men of Scotland and the Welsh [Strathclyde Britons], and the Saxons'. This may have been a second rise to power by Eric leading the Viking forces, or alternatively, he may have simply stepped in to grab power after the defeat. Eric's second reign was again short-lived and in 954 AD he was once more expelled by his Northumbrians subjects. There may have been another Viking king based at York around this time, but the details remain obscure except for coins minted in his name of Eltangerht.

As with Olaf's kingship, Eric's reigns clearly involved Archbishop Wulfstan as the leading Northumbrian churchman and major political force. The detailed relationships between Wulfstan and either Eric on the one hand, or King Eadred on the other, are unclear. However, it is implied that the retaliatory attack on Ripon, which had little real military significance, was intended as a blow against the archbishop in York and a warning of worse to come.

The possible roles and intrigues involving Wulstan from his base in York are part-evidenced from the witness lists of Anglo-Saxon charters. These indicate when or if Wulfstan attended King Eadred's court, and if it was as archbishop in his own right or as a diplomat to aid negotiations between two kings. These records suggest that between 938 AD and 941 AD, which is from the Battle of Brunanburh in 937 AD to the recovery of the Five Danelaw Boroughs in 942 AD, Wulfstan did not attest Anglo-Saxon royal charters. It appears that he began doing so around the time of the 942 AD negotiations.

During the turbulent years of AD 947 and 948 the charters have intermittent gaps suggesting the archbishop was absent from his attestation role. Then the numbers of charters declined because Eadred suffered poor health, during a critical period for understanding the major events between 950 and 954 AD. Wulfstan was at the English court in 950 AD, but apparently not during 951, the omission of his name from five charters during that year implying his support for the Viking Olaf against the claims of Ealdred. For Eric's reign (952 to 954 AD) the situation is less clear, though as Eric started the period of his second reign in York, Wulfstan was arrested by Eadred and tried at Iudanbyrig which is probably today's Jedburgh. Following Eric's death, Wulfstan was restored to office but with Dorchester as his episcopal seat a safe distance from his political power base of York. Wulfstan subsequently died at Oundle in Northamptonshire in December 956 AD, and was buried there. Oscytel, a kinsman of Oda, then became Archbishop of York.

Eric Bloodaxe is a very significant figure in terms of the political and military history of York, but he remains obstinately obscure. Indeed, the extent to which the various successions to the York throne were purely northern affairs or involved the active participation of English Mercia and Wessex is open to debate. Similarly, the accounts of Eric's death suggest complex issues and interactions in national politics. Accounts state that Eric was driven out and slain by Maccus, son of Onlaf. The *Flores historiarum* by Roger of Wendover and written in the 1200s, noted that 'King Eric was treacherously killed by Earl Maccus in a certain lonely place which is called Stainmore, with his son Haeric and his brother Ragnald, betrayed by Earl Oswulf; and then afterward King Eadred ruled in these districts'. The location of his betrayal was Stainmore which used to be in Westmorland, Cumbria, Stainmore Pass or Gap being the main pass through the northern Pennines marking the boundary between Cumbria in the west and Durham in the east. In Eric's time the mountains were traversed by an old Roman road, approximately the modern A66, and running from York to Catterick, then north-westward from Catterick to Carlisle. Perhaps Eric was following this route to Strathclyde or even the Hebrides as possible destinations.

Oswulf, central to this plot, was the high reeve of northern Northumbria with his influence based around Bamburgh and amounting roughly to the by then defunct kingdom of Bernicia. The incentive for Oswulf was to extend and consolidate his influence over this area. Accounts state that the province of Northumbria was subsequently administered by earls, and record that Oswulf was appointed Earl of Northumbria the year following Eric's murder. The man who actually killed Eric was Maccus, son of Onlaf (Anlaf), but we know little about him though it is suggested that he may have been of a Norse-Gaelic family based in the Border country between England and Scotland.

The death of Eric is mentioned in various histories and sagas but with different characters and scenarios; several interpretations suggest the last stand in a battle following pursuit by his enemies after deposition. It may be that Eric was assassinated as he fled into exile, perhaps seeking support for his claim to the York throne from northern and western territories. It is also unknown whether Oswulf himself was actually responsible for Eric's expulsion, or whether he was expected by Eric to grant him safe passage and maybe an escort for the journey. It is conjecture as to whether Maccus was part of an escort or perhaps ambushed his victims. Set as dialogue between Bragi, Odin, and fallen heroes, a poem was commissioned to commemorate Eric's death and his deeds. This recounts Eric's arrival in Valhalla with five other kings to receive a fine welcome from Odin and his companions. Odin speaks of eagerly awaiting Eric's arrival since 'many lands with his sword he has reddened'. Sigmund, a famous Norse hero greets Eric with, 'Hail now, Eric here you shall be welcome; brave hero, enter the hall.'

Although this poem is clearly strongly pagan in content, it may be that Eric died a Christian. While we have no specific evidence of his religious beliefs, when accepted and consecrated as king at York, it was almost certainly through Archbishop Wulfstan as kingmaker. Conversion to Christianity must have been one condition to taking up royal office. Indeed, the earlier Irish Norse kings Olaf and Ragnald were ejected by Wulfstan because they deserted the faith. The enigmatic Eric Bloodaxe who died in AD 954 was once a mighty and subsequently famous or infamous warrior and the last king of York. We get a flavour in these accounts of the power of the archbishop in York and the northern bishops as 'warrior bishops'.

In 954, the Viking kingdom of Northumbria was fully integrated into the greater kingdom of England, the Kingdom of Northumbria becoming an Earldom of England under the royal House of Wessex. At this point the title King of Jórvík became redundant and was replaced by the Earl of York, created in 960 AD. The city itself continued to thrive and around 1000 AD had an urban population second only to London. While some early earls of York were of Viking descent like their predecessor Jórvík kings, after the Conquest in

Warrior Bishops

As men of God, it was considered unacceptable for bishops or archbishops to use swords in battle and so to draw blood. However, it seems to have been okay for a man of the cloth to wield a mace or club and so bludgeon an opponent. The northern bishops in England were famously important in controlling the region and in defending against Scottish incursions. They held power in both the church and in secular matters, sometime being referred to as prince-bishops. Tenth-century Wulfstan, Archbishop of York, was an example of a northern cleric wielding huge political influence as a kingmaker and power-broker.

William the Conqueror's half-brother Odo of Bayeux was both Earl of Kent and Bishop of Bayeux, and for a time, the second in power to the king of England. He is depicted in the Bayeux Tapestry wielding a club. Odo is perhaps not the best example of a warrior bishop although he was one of the major examples of the genre; it was said that his considerable riches were the result of extortion and robbery, his ambition boundless, and his morals lax.

1066, they were followed by Normans. As we see later, William the Conqueror put an end to York's final claims to independence and imposed his power with a garrisoned castle. The Earldom of York was finally abolished by King Henry II in the twelfth century, and the title Duke of York was created in 1341. This title merged with the Crown itself when the 4th Duke became King Edward IV. Since that time, the title of Duke of York has generally been bestowed on the second son of the reigning king or queen.

The Viking settlement of York had a huge impact but since the Danes built mostly in timber, the actual remains did not always survive. There is an Old Norse place-name of Konungsgurth', or King's Court, recorded in the late fourteenth century and close to the west gatehouse of the old Roman encampment. Today this is King's Square and may suggest a former site of a Viking royal palace. Certainly new streets of timber houses were constructed between around 900 and 935 AD as the city sprawled outward. Some remains were preserved in anaerobic clay subsoils underlying parts of the old city, and this Viking heritage is celebrated and displayed at the Jorvic Museum. Even after the Norman Conquest, the Danish Vikings still attempted to recapture their former Northumbrian kingdom and its capital city.

Saxons, Vikings & Normans

In a turbulent period during the middle of the eleventh century, York was central to international power struggles in Britain and across the North Sea. Indeed, in England, York was a determining factor in the ultimate outcome of the Norman invasion of 1066 AD. A century after Eric's demise, Viking invaders with Northumbrian allies were victorious at the Battle of Fulford, when, on 20th September 1066, King Harald III of Norway (Harald Hardrada), and the banished English Tostig Godwinson, defeated the northern earls Edwin and Morcar. However, the tables were turned at the Battle of Stamford Bridge on 25th September 1066 when the English army under King Harold Godwinson routed the invaders. Nevertheless, considering the Battle of Hastings and the Norman Conquest which followed, this was something of a Pyrrhic victory. These turns of events had major ramifications for York and its people.

The Battle of Fulford

The Battle of Fulford or of Gate Fulford fought on the outskirts of York, has been overshadowed by the other great battles of 1066 at Stamford Bridge and Hastings. The sequence of events flowing from the defeat of the northern earls at Fulford led, a few weeks later, to the Norman Conquest of Britain. The Battle of Fulford was fought on the outskirts of the village of Fulford near York, when King Harald III of Norway, also known as Harald Hardrada (in Old Norse meaning 'hard ruler') and his English ally, Tostig Godwinson, fought and defeated the northern earls Edwin and Morcar. Tostig was Harold Godwinson's banished brother and had allied with King Harald of Norway and possibly William, Duke of Normandy, but there is no record of the reasoning behind his invasion. Fulford was a decisive victory for the Viking army. While the northern earls could have remained behind the protective walls of York they instead met the Viking army across the river. All day the English desperately tried to break the Viking shield-wall but to no avail. Tostig and Earl Morcar had a long-standing enmity, the latter having displaced the former as Earl of Northumbria and this meeting must have brought emotions to a bitter head.

The context to the contestation of the English throne was that the Anglo-Saxon king, Edward the Confessor, had died without an heir on 5th January 1066. This left the sole surviving member of the royal family as Edgar, the young son of Edward Atheling. So on 6th January, the day of Edward's funeral, Harold Godwinson, the Earl of Wessex and the head of the most powerful Saxon dynasty, made his way to London, to be crowned as king by Aldred, Archbishop of York in Westminster Abbey. Harold had been elected as king by the Witenagemot whose members were already gathered to celebrate the feast of Epiphany. A complication was that two powerful earls, brothers Edwin of Mercia and Morcar of Northumbria, came forward to challenge Harold's authority. It seems that Harold went north to confront them and resolve the issue, which was sorted by him marrying their sister, Edith, the widow of Griffith of Wales, and thus securing the support of two very powerful allies. Furthermore, the alliance with Edwin and Morcar, Harold strengthened his position in northern England and York itself.

However, while Harold was the senior Saxon claimant, his unpredictable and violent brother Tostig felt that he too was the legitimate heir to the Crown. Exiled to Flanders because of his behaviour in England, in May 1066, Tostig invaded, gathering additional forces along the way and sailing to the Humber to battle the forces of Edwin, the Earl of Mercia. This foray ended in defeat for Tostig and he retreated north to the protection of King Malcolm of Scotland and to make an alliance with another claimant to the English throne, Harald Hardrada, King of Norway. It may also be that Tostig travelled to Normandy to ask for assistance from William, Duke of Normandy, but the latter was unwilling to offer support. Ultimately, Tostig and his supporters allied with Hardrada and fought side by side at the Battle of Fulford.

For Hardrada, Tostig was a useful ally not only being the brother of his main adversary, King Harold, but because he had a good knowledge of the country and the terrain. In August 1066, the Norwegians sailed for Orkney, arriving in September. Here they collected supplies and met with Tostig, who brought additional soldiers and ships. Together they sailed round the coast and up the great Humber Estuary. They entered the mouth of the Humber on 18th September and from here the combined force made its way up the River Ouse and toward their first objective, the strategically important City of York. Having disembarked from their ships, the armies moved speedily on toward York and on 20th September 1066, were facing the forces of the earls Edwin and Morcar.

Earl Edwin had brought soldiers to the east of the city in the expectation of an invasion by the Norwegian force and the conflict began with English troops moving wide to safeguard their flanks. For the Saxons, on their right was the River Ouse, and on the left was a swampy area called Fordland. Strategically this position taken up by the earls had disadvantages, one being that Hardrada held the higher ground and thus had a vantage point from which to oversee the battle. Furthermore, should one flank of the Saxon army falter, the other flank would also be in trouble. An additional problem was that while the marshes helped protect the Saxon position, they also meant that if the Vikings broke through, there was no easy retreat.

Hadrada and Tostig approached the field along three routes from the south and they assembled opposite the Anglo-Saxons; their force arrived piecemeal and it would take a good few hours for all of their troops to assemble. The least battle-hardened Vikings were set to the right and the more experienced soldiers occupied the riverbank. The Saxon force attacked the Viking army to pre-empt its full deployment with Earl Morcar's soldiers forcing the weaker Viking line back into the marshes. However, this early success was not enough to carry the day and the Viking force was now supported by their better troops, the right flank attacking the centre and additional men moving along the riverbank. Despite a numerical advantage the Saxons were being made to concede territory, and Earl Edwin's men defending the riverbank were cut off by the marsh from the rest of the army. They now moved back to York for a final stand. On the beck, the Saxon troops were hard-pressed and a further Viking incursion with fresh men meant a third front had now developed; now outnumbered and outmanoeuvred, the York army was beaten. The earls Edwin and Morcar survived the conflict and with York surrendering to the Vikings it was negotiated that there would be no forced entry or looting, Tostig presumably viewing York as his own future capital. Hostages were given and the Norwegian force fell back some seven miles eastward to Stamford Bridge.

Estimates suggest the Viking force at Fulford numbered about 10,000 with 6,000 actually used in the battle, and the Saxons had around 5,000. Both sides suffered heavy casualties estimated at perhaps 15 per cent fatalities so a total of about 1,650 and much of the fighting power of the combined Mercian and Northumbrian armies was destroyed or compromised.

With news of the defeat, King Harold decided to force-march his own troops from London to York, a distance of 190 miles. This strategic decision meant he arrived near York within a week of the Battle of Fulford, thus surprising the Viking army and defeating them at the Battle of Stamford Bridge. However, in the meantime William, Duke of Normandy, landed his own army in Sussex on the now undefended English south coast and in response Harold marched back down to the south where the two armies met near Hastings. Harold probably hoped that in catching William off-guard he might repeat the success of Stamford Bridge. The twin battles at Gate Fulford and then at Stamford Bridge, fought within a single week of each other, must have significantly weakened Harold's available forces at Hastings just three weeks later. Without the two battles near York, the outcome of Hastings might well have been very different. As it was, the strategic role of York probably changed English history forever.

The Battle of Stamford Bridge

One of the key conflicts in English history but overshadowed by the subsequent Battle of Hastings, the Battle of Stamford Bridge took place at the village of the same name in the East Riding of Yorkshire. The conflict, on 25th September 1066, was between a Saxon army under King Harold Godwinson and the invading Viking force of King Harald

Hardrada of Norway and Harold's brother Tostig. Following a fierce battle, both Hardrada and Tostig were dead along with many of their men. Harold carried the day only to be defeated shortly afterwards by William of Normandy. Stamford Bridge has been viewed as symbolic of the end of Viking influence or at least the 'Viking Age' in northern England and in York itself. Nevertheless, there were significant Scandinavian campaigns in Britain and Ireland in following decades as warring factions jostled for overall power, the Vikings clearly hoping to regain their lost kingdom. The Danish King Sweyn Estrithson made incursions from 1069 to 1070 and the Norwegian King Magnus Barefoot did likewise in 1098 and then again from 1102 to 1103. In truth though, the Viking influence was never again as it once had been.

There is some dispute over the exact location of the battle at Stamford Bridge, as indeed there is about the site of the Battle of Hastings. It is almost certain that there was a bridge over the River Derwent close to the present-day village, and that at least a part of the battle centred on or about this point. The suggestion is also that there was a fording point close to the modern bridge site. So while local tradition puts the battlefield east of the River Derwent and just south-east of the modern town, in a location called Battle Flats, the precise position is unknown. The Viking army's location as the battle began is uncertain though it is believed that the force was split into two groups, some on the west bank of the Derwent but most on the east bank. They may even have been on the move heading back from Stamford Bridge toward York along the old Roman road.

It may be that there was a two-pronged attack by Harold's forces via the ford and possibly an older Roman bridge about a mile to the south of Stamford Bridge, utilizing

Stamford Bridge and the site of the famous river crossing in 1066.

The annihilation of the Vikings at the Battle of Stamford Bridge.

two roads to the battle-site from York. On the east bank of the River Derwent, from the crossing, the topography rises quickly up to about 100 feet at High Catton. Here is the only higher ground in this low-lying, predominantly flat landscape – a strong defensive position for the Viking army. However, it seems Hadrada and Tostig were caught unawares by the sudden appearance of Harold's army as he came around the Gate Helmsley ridge and swept downhill toward their troops.

Clearly, the unexpected arrival of Saxons took the Vikings by surprise and their response to imminent assault was to deploy rapidly into a defensive circle, presumably with a traditional Viking shield-wall. Topographic details become important since if they were on Battle Flats, this deployment by the Viking troops would make little sense, but located east of the Derwent the defensive circle would be a logical move. It seems that by the time the main English army arrived, Hardrada's men on the west bank were either dead or retreating back across the bridge or ford. The Saxon advance was held up by the river-crossing pinch-point with a local legend as recounted by the *Anglo-Saxon Chronicle* of a giant Norse axe-man armed with a Dane-axe blocking the crossing and single-handedly stalling the whole Saxon army. It was said that he felled around forty Saxon warriors before eventually being defeated by a Saxon soldier who floated under the bridge in a half-barrel. He apparently thrust his spear through gaps between the planks in the bridge and skewered the unfortunate Viking. Of course, this story requires a bridge rather than just a ford.

The time taken to cross the river allowed most of the Viking force to form a shield-wall in anticipation of the Saxon assault. Harold Godwinson's soldiers now crossed the river and formed a line somewhat short of the Viking shield-wall; they locked shields and charged at the invaders. The action spread way beyond the river crossing, the battle raging for hours. The need for haste meant the Vikings had not had time to put on full armour and this was now a big disadvantage. After several hours the Viking army began to break up and the Saxons were able to press on through the shield-wall. Now outflanked and their leaders killed, Hardrada with an arrow through the windpipe and Tostig slain too, the Viking force fell apart and was effectively annihilated.

As the battle progressed, the Vikings were joined by fresh soldiers left with the ships at Riccall. These new troops were led by Hardrada's prospective son-in-law, Eystein Orre. In their haste to get to the battlefield, it is suggested that some of the men collapsed and died of exhaustion. Those remaining however were fully armed for battle and their brutal counter-attack, known from Viking sagas as 'Orre's Storm', checked the Saxon advance. However, now heavily outnumbered the Vikings were soon overwhelmed, Orre himself killed, and the Viking army routed. Finally, chased by Saxon troops, many fleeing Norsemen were drowned attempting to cross rivers. It was said that so many died in such a small area that the field was still whitened with bleached bones more than fifty years following the slaughter.

Eventually, King Harold Godwinson and the few surviving Vikings agreed a truce. These included Harald's son Olaf and the Earl of Orkney, Paul Thorfinnsson who were allowed to leave after pledging to never again attack England. The losses endured by the Vikings were colossal and from the fleet of over three hundred ships which had arrived, just twenty-four were enough to carry away the survivors. These few headed back to

William the Conqueror.

Orkney for the winter, and the following spring, Hardrada's son, Olaf returned home to Norway which kingdom was divided between him and his brother Magnus who had been left to govern the homeland during the invasion of England.

The final throw of the dice in this epic time in English history was when, only three days after Stamford Bridge, on 28th September 1066, William, Duke of Normandy landed in Pevensey Bay, Sussex, on the southern English coast. Exhausted from the battle with the Vikings and having suffered major casualties in two huge conflicts, King Harold and the Saxons now had to force-march south to meet the Norman army. Less than three weeks following victory in the Battle of Stamford Bridge, on 14th October 1066, the Saxon army was heavily defeated by the Normans. King Harold II fell in action at the Battle of Hastings, the Norman conquest of England was underway, and made so much easier by heavy losses of the elite Saxon military commanders and ruling classes from three massive battles in about a month.

4. HARRYING OF THE NORTH

Victory at the Battle of Hastings did not guarantee William control of England. The rebellious North had to be brought into line, which it was, ruthlessly, in the winter of 1069 AD. An obvious focus of northern identity and independence, York was the target of Norman imposition and reprisals against opposition.

The Battle of Hastings, the most famous event of the Norman Conquest, was only the opening engagement in the invaders' consolidation of power in England. For several years afterwards, the country was riven by internal conflict as the Normans fought to extend their rule, climaxing in a notorious campaign known today as the 'Harrying of the North'.

The Harrying, sometimes described as genocide, took place over the winter of 1069/70, and saw William's troops lay waste to large parts of Yorkshire and neighbouring shires. Entire villages were razed, their inhabitants killed, livestock slaughtered, and food stores destroyed. The scorched-earth policy became a defining aspect of the Norman Conquest. This was not merely from a military and political perspective but also in shaping modern perceptions of the Normans as tyrannical and merciless warriors. But why were such brutal measures considered necessary and why was the North particularly targeted?

By the winter of 1069, the imposed Norman war-machine had been active across England for over three years. Throughout 1067 and 1068 there was a succession of localized revolts such as in Devon, Kent, Herefordshire, the midland earldom of Mercia, and the Fenlands though each was speedily and brutally suppressed. There were incursions by overseas forces, particularly Vikings, and these were similarly repelled as the Normans consolidated power. Across the new kingdom fortifications were quickly established with motte and bailey castles built of wood and only gradually converted to stone. Locations for these structures included major strategic towns such as Warwick, Nottingham, Lincoln, Huntingdon, Cambridge, and of course, York itself. The objective was to suppress rebellion and impose iron control. By early 1069, William's influence extended to York and its immediate environs but not much farther. It was clear that here in the unruly north was the greatest threat.

King William's first attempts to bring Norman rule to the North was through the appointment of native Saxon earls (firstly Earl Copsig and then Earl Gospatric) as governors; both attempts ended in failure. In 1067, Copsig was assassinated by a rival, and in 1068, Earl Gospatric joined the rebels. William took his army north into Northumbria, arriving in York during summer 1068 but the opposition slipped away, and some, including Edgar Atheling, took refuge with the Scottish king Malcolm III. Finally in desperation, in January 1069, William despatched one of his Norman lords, Robert Cumin or Robert de Comines, to deal with the situation. He headed northward with an army to reconquer the region by force. However, this too failed when they were ambushed. In spite of warnings of rebellion from Bishop Ethelwin, Robert, with a party of Norman soldiers, rode into Durham on 28th January 1069, only to find himself surrounded and he and his men were slaughtered.

Aerial view of York Castle in 1928 but still giving a feel of the scale of the medieval fortification.

Things got worse for the Normans and during the summer as William faced the prospect of all his foes advancing at the same time. Leading these was a coalition of Northumbrian noblemen with Earl Gospatric and led by the royal claimant, 17-year-old Edgar Atheling. Following Harold's death in 1066, the latter was briefly crowned king in London. As the last legitimate Wessex claimant to the throne, there was encouragement

From the establishment of Alan Rufus, St Mary's Abbey Gatehouse and Lodgeby F. Place, about 1700.

enough to trigger Saxon and Viking uprisings which stretched to breaking point the Norman grip on northern England. Edgar Atheling had sought assistance from Sweyn II, the king of Denmark, himself a nephew of King Canute. Under the command of his sons, Sweyn despatched a fleet of ships which passed along the English east coast to help local rebels recapture York. By August, the Northumbrian uprisings were supported by a Danish Viking invasion fleet of 200 to 300 ships which arrived in the Humber. The Saxons and Vikings forged an alliance and jointly laid siege to York. Probably coincidental rather than in any way coordinated, the northern revolts seemed to catalyse trouble for William on the borders of Wales when a local thegn called Eadric had joined with Welsh kings and Saxons from Cheshire to rise up against the Normans. In south-west England, Devon and Cornwall were also in rebellion, and this was growing to a crisis point for the Norman conquerors. Events in York were clearly an encouragement for others to follow, and as the city fell to the resistance, the rebels killed the guardian of the castle plus many soldiers. Maybe encouraged by ongoing conflict in the northern shires, sporadic uprisings were breaking out across the country and Norman barons were sent out to suppress problems in Dorset, Shrewsbury, and Devon. William himself addressed rebellions in the Midlands and Staffordshire. The Normans sent William's deputies to south-west England while the king himself suppressed revolts in the Welsh borders, before defeating the Midlands rebels at Stafford. He could then head north.

William's riposte was brutal and speedy as he returned to York to deal with rebels who were either killed or fled. It was recorded in the chronicles that, in the winter of

1069, King William led his troops across northern England, especially Yorkshire, to quash a rebellion that involved the sacking of York. William had marched his army from Nottingham to York in order to engage the rebels in battle.

A forgotten link to this episode was that during the journey to York the Normans found the River Aire crossing at modern-day Pontefract (the name meaning 'broken bridge' in Latin) blockaded by Saxon and Viking resistance and they had indeed broken the bridge. The rebels held the northern bank in some force, but this did not deflect the Norman advance for long. (After the Harrying, in 1070, Ilbert de Lacy was gifted Pontefract by William as reward for his services and he built the formidable castle on the high rocky outcrop above the modern town.)

When William's army reached York, the rebels mostly dispersed to hideouts in the hills and woods of Yorkshire, and Edgar fled back to Scotland. The Danes were spending the winter on their ships in the Humber, and to ease the pressure slightly, after negotiations, William paid them to leave. Thus depleted, the remaining rebels now avoided direct confrontation. William's response to their tactic of guerrilla warfare was harsh: to lay waste to villages and the countryside, and to towns and cities particularly York, thus starving the rebels into submission. He then imposed a lordship of Norman aristocrats to keep order into the future with York a key strategic stronghold.

With the Danish Vikings gone without a fight, William was eager to bring other matters to an effective conclusion. Unable to force a key battle, the strategy of 'wasting' and resultant starvation came into play. William's troops destroyed the rebels' support and especially their food. This policy, described by some as genocide, was implemented during the winter of 1069/70. William was in York for Christmas 1069, contemporary writers

Layerthorpe Postern and Towers from the River Foss, by J. Halfpenny 1807.

Bootham Bar and the Minster early 1900s.

describing his acts as immensely cruel, a 'stain upon his soul'. The Anglo-Norman chronicler in the early 1100s, Orderic Vitalis, described the 'Harrying of the North':

> The King stopped at nothing to hunt his enemies. He cut down many people and
> destroyed homes and land. Nowhere else had he shown such cruelty. This made a real
> change. To his shame, William made no effort to control his fury, punishing the innocent
> with the guilty. He ordered that crops and herds, tools and food be burned to ashes. More
> than 100,000 people perished of starvation. I have often praised William in this book,
> but I can say nothing good about this brutal slaughter. God will punish him.

As the Norman army went north from the River Aire, the countryside all along their route
was wasted, crops and settlements destroyed and rebels forced into hiding. Then, in early
1070 he divided his forces into smaller units despatched to burn, loot, and terrify the
populace. A commentator, Florence of Worcester, wrote that 'from the Humber to the
Tees, William's men burnt whole villages and slaughtered the inhabitants. Food stores and
livestock were destroyed so that anyone surviving the initial massacre would succumb to
starvation over the winter. The survivors were reduced to cannibals.' Refugees from the
slaughter dispersed far and wide with some recorded as far off as Worcestershire. As a

sign of desperation local people buried hordes of coins to keep them safe for happier, more settled times.

The consequences for York and the North were deep and long-lasting as evidenced by the 1086 entries for Yorkshire and the North Riding in the *Domesday Book* still noting extensive waste land as '*wasteas est*' or '*hoc est vast*' (i.e. it is wasted) for settlement after settlement. A frightening total of around 60 per cent of all recorded estates were waste and 66 per cent of vills included 'wasted manors'. Beyond the sheer destruction of the lands, any remaining prosperous parts of Yorkshire had reductions in value amounting to about 60 per cent of their pre-Conquest value. At the end of the wasting only around a quarter of the population remained alive, a loss of approximately 150,000 people and they had lost about 80,000 oxen from the plough-teams. Symeon of Durham wrote that 'no village remained inhabited between York and Durham and the countryside remained empty and uncultivated for nine years'. Since the total population of England at the time was only a little over two million it is possible the figures are exaggerated, but nonetheless losses were devastating.

Alongside the Norman wasting, some Domesday manors in the North were destroyed by raiding parties of Vikings, Scots, and in some cases the rebels themselves. The Norman army was relatively small, and we know of the sacking of York for example, by the combined rebel forces. The overall impact of the Norman forces on York and its surroundings

The inside of Clifford's Tower at York Castle, the scene of various horrific incidents in history.

has been debated especially since most of William's troops were establishing and defending castles in south England and Wales. Could William have brought in sufficient troops to cause so much damage? Were the records partly misinterpreted or exaggerated for effect? William himself was only based in York for around three months so there was a limit to the destruction he could wreak. However, while the chroniclers and even *Domesday* might exaggerate, the documentation suggests a region utterly devastated. From William's perspective the intention was probably threefold: suppress the current uprisings, remove the resistance from its strongholds, and finally, send a clear message to would-be Saxon or Viking rebels. York was the example for the rest, as it is said in French, '*pour encourager les autres*' – to encourage the others.

Aiming to end once and for all the cycles of uprisings by removing the basic sustenance for any would-be rebels, the operation was efficient and effective. Norman forces operated across a hundred-mile radius of countryside from York north to the River Tyne. Twelfth-century writer John of Worcester stated 'that food was so scarce in the aftermath that people were reduced to eating not just horses, dogs and cats but also human flesh.' Many died directly while others simply starved in the aftermath or suffered fatal diseases. The message was clear: with the Battle of Hastings only the beginning, with the Harrying of the North, and especially of York itself, punishment for rebellion would be swift, decisive and brutal.

The next step in William's plan to bring York and the North into line was wholesale replacement of Anglo-Saxon aristocracy by Normans. So in 1071, William appointed yet another Earl of Northumbria, and William Walcher as the first non-English Bishop of Durham. The result for York and the surrounding shires was the imposition of new, mostly Norman aristocracy. There was also Alan Rufus, one of William's faithful Breton allies who was given a major holding in North Yorkshire, noted in *Domesday* as 'the Hundred of the Land of Count Alan', and which became Richmondshire. Rufus governed his lands as a small principality with almost no other Norman lords given any entitlement. Interestingly, and counter-intuitive to what had gone before, Rufus kept on the surviving Anglo-Danish lords or their heirs. However, despite the success of Alan Rufus's appointment it is clear that the troubles were still not fully quelled. In 1079, the Scots were raiding into Northumbria and escaping with booty and slaves, but Walcher seemed unable or unwilling to intervene. Consequently, in 1080, William Walcher, Bishop of Durham, was killed by local Northumbrians petitioning about various wrongdoings and troubles. A trigger for unrest was the murder of one of Walcher's senior counsellors of old Northumbrian lineage by rival Normans. The Bishop had agreed to meet the protestors and for safety travelled with around a hundred retainers. On 14th May 1080, they met at Gateshead, with Eadulf Rus the leader of the Northumbrian kinsmen, and a petition of wrongs committed was presented to him. However, Walcher promptly rejected the submission and so the infuriated Northumbrians turned on the Normans who sought refuge in a nearby church. This led the Northumbrians to set fire to the wooden building with some of the party dying within and Walcher and the rest of his group forced into the open to be slaughtered by the protestors.

In response to these latest issues, William despatched his own half-brother Odo, Bishop of Bayeux with an army to once again harry the Northumbrian countryside. Odo's troops

The Harrying of the North, as depicted on the Bayeux Tapestry.

destroyed villages and crops across a wide swathe of land from York to Durham and north beyond the River Tees. The Norman soldiers ransacked Durham Monastery and many surviving Northumbrian nobles were forced into exile.

However, Rufus remained successful and exercised patronage in York itself, in 1088, founding St Mary's Abbey. A shrewd operator and now hugely influential in York and the North, by the time of *Domesday* in 1086, Alan Rufus was among the most powerful and richest men in Norman England.

York itself was badly damaged by Norman reprisals in the so-called 'wasting of the North'. Nevertheless, the city eventually settled again to become important as the main administrative centre in Yorkshire, one of the major ecclesiastical establishments in England, and a growing urban hub for the region. In early medieval times, York emerged as a strategic crossing point on the River Ouse. It was sufficiently far north for royal visits, a stronghold of power in northern England, and a base for the Council of the North. Location was an important consideration in a medieval England often torn apart by civil strife and unrest, with the ever-present threat of incursions from the Scots to the north. Furthermore, internal English struggles triggered allegiances with the Scots or opportunistic raids southward across the border. In the short-term, King Malcolm of Scotland married into William's family and accepted his status as a vassal of the now English king. The last Wessex royal claimant Edgar also submitted to William's rule and overlordship.

5. POST-CONQUEST YORK & ENGLAND AT WAR

Following the Conquest there was supposedly a time of peace and in subsequent centuries there were periods actually called 'civil wars'. Yet, a glance at the history of York and the North suggests major and minor conflicts and incursions from Scotland south into England were pretty much the norm. Ongoing dynastic feuds and scrambling for control of the English Crown continued throughout the period that followed William I's death with wars between two of his sons, Robert and William Rufus, who became William II.

York was forever involved as the key position to control the North, even if the epicentre of struggles lay in the south of England or in Normandy. For example, in the war between English King Stephen and Empress Matilda during a time called appropriately 'The Anarchy', in 1138, the Battle of the Standard took place near Northallerton in North Yorkshire. This was one of the major conflicts of the period when the English forces of King Stephen repelled a Scottish army on 22nd August on Cowton Moor. Scotland's King David I had crossed the border into northern England with an army of 16,000 men. The Scottish army, led by King David I (King of Scotland and Prince of Cumbria), had twofold intentions: to support his niece Matilda's claim to the English throne in opposition to King Stephen who was married to another of his nieces, and to add further land to the Scottish kingdom beyond gains already made.

King Stephen was taken up with battling rebel barons in southern England and sent a small force mostly of mercenaries. The English army commanded by William of Aumale with mainly local militia and baronial troops from Yorkshire and the north Midlands were supported by York's Archbishop Thurstan helping raise troops by preaching that to battle the Scots was to do God's work. Consequently, the central point of the English position was marked by a mast mounted on a cart bearing a sacred *pyx*, or standard, from the consecrated host and flying the consecrated banners of the minsters of York, Beverley and Ripon. It was this standard which gave its name to the battle.

By the time of the contest, David's forces had taken much of Northumberland apart from major castles at Wark and Bamburgh. Then, advancing beyond the River Tees toward York, early on 22nd August 1138, the Scots found the English army drawn up on open fields two miles north of Northallerton. They established four 'lines' to attack the English; the first sortie failed as it pitched unarmoured spearmen against armoured men who included dismounted knights with supporting fire from archers. So-called 'arrow-storming' tactics were important in the defeat of the Scots during the battle. Perhaps God had been listening to the archbishop and the bishops as the Scottish lines broke following fierce hand-to-hand fighting. It took just three hours for the Scottish army to fall back in disarray, leaving small groups of knights and men-at-arms around King David and his son Prince Henry. The latter led a brave charge with mounted knights and then he and the king left the field in reasonably good order, but their army had suffered severe losses both during the battle and the flight from the field. The Battle of the Standard was something of a Pyrrhic victory as the English army did not harry the fleeing Scots away from the battlefield, the Yorkshire-based force not taking full advantage of the rout and thus many Scottish soldiers escaped. King David fell back to Carlisle where he gathered his fragmented troops once more, and they remained in control of much of the north for the next twenty years.

A truce was agreed and oddly the Scots were allowed to continue the siege of Wark Castle and the fortress finally fell. Furthermore, although he had lost the Battle of Northallerton, David gained most of the territory that he was after and had been offered before his army crossed the River Tees into North Yorkshire. David held the lands throughout the period of the Anarchy, but when he died in 1153 AD, his successor, Malcolm IV of Scotland handed them back to the English king, Henry II.

For much of this period, lands north of York and mostly governed from the city, were a source of trouble and dispute. Powerful northern barons and opportunistic Scottish lairds and monarchs in search of England's wealth, combined to make this a disputed territory for many centuries. Aggression and raiding were countered by reprisals and counter-attacks. Indeed, following the defeat of the Scottish royalty and nobility by the 'Hammer of the Scots' Edward I (1239–1307), the response after Edward's death was to strike deep into England with monarchs such as Robert Bruce. Born in 1284, Edward II's reign (1307–1327), was an important and significant period in the military history of York.

Clifford's Tower, York.

During the reign of Edward II, it was almost a seasonal pursuit to raid south across the border and in 1318 and 1319, the Scots pressed on into Yorkshire to burn and loot Northallerton, Wetherby, Knaresborough, and Boroughbridge. They spared Ripon on payment of a ransom of 1,000 marks. Then, while Edward II was taken up with trying to recapture the strategic border town of Berwick-on-Tweed, captured by Robert Bruce, a Scottish army pushed farther southward toward York. At this point, with its men seconded to take part in the Berwick campaign, the city was largely undefended. However, the Scots still failed to take York and, unable to enter the city and capture Queen Isabella, the soldiers turned for home. Nevertheless, their anticipated return to Scotland proved more eventful than expected because the Archbishop of York had now raised an army of around 10,000 men. This large but mostly untrained force set off in a brave but ultimately foolhardy pursuit of the Scots, the armies meeting at Myton near Boroughbridge, where the River Ure joins the River Swale. Although they outnumbered the Scots, the English army was inexperienced and ill-equipped. After crossing the river at Myton Bridge, they were attacked and began to flee but with Scottish troops controlling the strategic bridge, the English were forced to hold their ground or brave the water. Since few could swim, many were drowned and others were slaughtered including around 200 monks, whose corpses were left on the field of battle. With their white habits drenched with blood, the conflict assumed the name of 'The White Battle'.

Boroughbridge

The Battle of Boroughbridge was not against the Scots, but between rebels led by the Earl of Lancaster and those loyal to Edward II of England. While it not part of the Wars of Scottish Independence, Boroughbridge was significant because of use of tactics developed during the Scottish conflict. The extensive deployment of foot soldiers as opposed to mounted cavalry, and the effective use of longbow archers were major developments in military tactics.

The Battle of Boroughbridge was fought on 16th March 1322 between rebellious barons led by the king's cousin, Thomas Earl of Lancaster, and King Edward II of England. The battle took place at Boroughbridge, close by the Great North Road and not far north-west of York. This was the culmination of a long period of conflict between the king and the barons, particularly his most powerful and wealthy subject, Earl Thomas. The latter was fleeing north after one of his closest allies had defected to the Crown and as his modest troop of around 700 men neared Boroughbridge they found the king's general, Sir Andrew Harclay, Earl of Carlisle (also de Harcla), holding the wooden bridge across the river. This presented Thomas with a serious dilemma: to either confront Harclay and attempt to take the crossing, or else turn south to face King Edward's own rapidly advancing army. Lancaster opted for the former which was to be his downfall, his Waterloo. Harclay's foot soldiers held the bridge from the northern side while further troops were set at a nearby ford. The latter included pikemen deployed in a 'schiltron' formation (a tight shield-wall or phalanx), something acquired from the Scots in the Scottish wars and effective against oncoming cavalry such as at Boroughbridge. Lancaster's rebels split into two columns: one led by the Earl of

Micklegate Bar by J. Halfpenny, 1807.

Hereford and Roger de Clifford attacked the bridge on foot, the second, led by Lancaster himself, attempted to cross the ford on horseback.

Accounts of the battle provided graphic and gory details such as Earl Hereford killed by a pikeman as he crossed the bridge. The foot soldier hiding beneath the bridge thrust his pike up between the wooden planks of the bridge and speared the Earl through his anus. With Roger de Clifford also severely injured, their column was in disarray and fell back. The Earl of Lancaster's group also fared badly and with heavy archery fire, his cavalry was halted before reaching the ford and had to retreat.

Having negotiated a truce with Harclay, Lancaster withdrew to the nearby town to regroup and assess the situation. However, things got worse for Lancaster as during the night many of his soldiers deserted, and the following day the Sheriff of York arrived from the south with additional forces. Harclay's soldiers armed with longbows massacred Lancaster's remaining troops and Earl Thomas, now greatly outnumbered and with no opportunity to retreat, had little choice but to surrender. He was captured and taken to York and following a show-trial at Pontefract, Edward II ordered that he be drawn, hanged and beheaded at Pontefract Castle.

This resounding victory enabled Edward to re-establish royal authority and cling to power for five more years. The battle had major impact on the latter years of the reign and was significant for the application of military tactics learned during the Scottish wars. This early use of the longbow led, twenty years later, to its devastating application in the French wars at Crécy, Poitiers, and Agincourt.

Old Byland

Relief for Edward Idid not last too long and soon afterwards he was again defeated by the Scots, this time at the Battle of Old Byland, Byland Moor, or Byland Abbey. This was a significant battle in October 1322 between English and Scottish troops as part of the ongoing Wars of Scottish Independence. With Boroughbridge heralding a new start for Edward with baronial opposition vanquished, it was a military high point in his reign. Probably emboldened by his rare victory, he set out on a final invasion of Scotland which ended in disaster for the English Crown.

When Edward began his military advance during early August, King Robert Bruce was ready and prepared. The usual Scottish tactics were brought into play with crops destroyed, livestock removed, and the Scottish army withdrawn beyond the River Forth to play a waiting game. Consequently, when the English arrived they found no food and no opposition. It was said that in the whole of Lothian the English found only one lame cow, sparking a remark from the Earl of Surrey that 'This is the dearest beef I ever saw. It surely has cost a thousand pounds and more!' As Edward marched on Edinburgh, at Leith the troops suffered sickness and hunger and were forced to retreat for want of food. Additionally, Edward's light horse troop was defeated by James de Douglas and few soldiers dared leave the ranks of the English army to forage for food because of harassment from the Scots. By the time the English army arrived back in Newcastle, rampant disease and starvation meant the army had to disband.

In a gesture of anger and defiance, as they retreated southward and back across the border, English troops destroyed both Holyrood Abbey in Edinburgh and the border abbeys of Melrose and Dryburgh. The invasion of Scotland achieved absolutely nothing but distress and acute embarrassment with worse to follow. The impact on English national morale of this ignominious retreat by their starving army was compared with the loss to the Scots at Bannockburn. But English retreat was not the end of this sorry saga since it heralded further Scottish attacks and incursions.

Robert Bruce and his army crossed the Solway in the west and then turned south-east toward Yorkshire and York. He brought with him many soldiers from Argyll and the Isles. The speed and boldness of this incursion south, known as 'The Great Raid of 1322', was a stark reminder to Edward of the dangers lying in wait even in his own kingdom. After his retreat from Scotland, the English monarch resided with Queen Isabella at Rievaulx Abbey in North Yorkshire, but the attack by Bruce, sudden and unexpected, meant that by mid-October there was little between them and a decisive royal prize. The only significant barrier was a large English force commanded by John of Brittany, the Earl of Richmond.

Earl John took a position on Scawton Moor, between Rievaulx and Byland Abbey. To ease him from this strong station on the high ground, the Scots employed tactics that had brought victory at the earlier Battle of the Pass of Brander. Lords Moray and Douglas attacked upslope toward the English while a troop of Highlanders climbed the cliffs to the side of the English flank to mount a Highland charge downslope and into Richmond's rear-guard. English resistance soon crumbled under this double assault and Old Byland became a rout. Numerous nobles including Henry de Sully, Grand Butler of France, Sir Ralph Cobham ('the best knight in England', Sir Thomas Ughtred, and Richmond himself were captured, with others killed on the battlefield or in flight.

As events unfolded, Edward, regarded as 'ever chicken hearted and luckless in war', made a rapid, undignified exit from Rievaulx; so hasty that he left his personal belongings behind. Following Byland, it was said the Scots became so fierce and their chiefs so daring, that the English before them were cowed, like a hare before the hounds. This battle in Yorkshire and close to York itself was a major victory for the Scots, and though on a far smaller scale, was the most significant since Bannockburn.

During this period of the Anglo-Scottish Wars and the reign of weak-willed Edward II, some of the most significant, yet today little-known, battles were fought in and around Yorkshire. For much of a forty-year period York itself was the functional working capital of the English kingdom and a forward base for major military operations. The royal court was at York and key functions of government, such as the exchequer or treasury, were based there. At this time, York was the lynchpin for national politics and warfare until, in the 1330s, Scotland and England reached a degree of relative peace, the city losing its significance as the war capital and the English government returned to London.

England at War with Itself

York flourished during the late medieval period, with the fourteenth and fifteenth centuries particularly prosperous. However, it was badly affected by two major English

R-construction of York Castle and the defences, about 1400, by Peter Russell.

civil wars, the Wars of the Roses being the first as internal struggles of the English monarchy ebbed and flowed.

The Wars of the Roses or More Correctly the 'Wars of the Cousins'

As with earlier times, the second half of the fifteenth century in England experienced ongoing political turmoil and periodic outbreak of civil war. The two would-be royal houses of York and Lancaster competed violently for control of the Crown, the war that was eventually called 'The War of The Roses' – the white rose of York versus the red rose of Lancaster – and that ran from 1455 to 1485. The conflict emerged only two years after the end of the Hundred Years' War with France. While the war is too complex to consider in detail here, it is central to York, the House of York and their place in military history. The first War of the Roses battle took place on 22nd May 1455, during the reign of Lancastrian King Henry VI (1422–61), and was called The First Battle of St. Albans. The result was a victory for the Yorkist army but also the start of a long and bloody civil war. Battles continued across England at various places over the subsequent period, examples being Blore Heath in Staffordshire in 1459, a Yorkist victory, and Ludford Bridge in Shropshire in 1459, a Lancastrian victory.

During 1460, there were several key events of the war, with the Lancastrian Henry VI engaging in numerous battles against the Yorkist armies led the Duke of York and the

Earl of Warwick. The Battle of Northampton on 10th July 1460 resulted in the capture of King Henry by the House of York; Henry suffered a mental breakdown and Richard Duke of York was appointed Regent of England. By October 1460, the Act of Accord named Richard Duke of York as King of England, taking the succession away from Henry's six-year old son in favour of Richard.

The Battle of Wakefield

However, Richard's reign was short-lived, as later that year, having taken up a strong position at Sandal Castle in the ancient administrative centre of Wakefield west of York, he sallied forth to lose catastrophically against the Lancastrians. Margaret of Anjou together with prominent pro-Lancastrian nobility was bitterly opposed to Richard's succession and had gathered an army. Lancastrian forces assembled around Kingston upon Hull were estimated at about fifteen thousand. Soon many of these had moved to near Pontefract and were actively pillaging Yorkshire estates held by both York and by the Earl of Salisbury. In dealing with these challenges to his authority as Protector or King, York sent his eldest son Edward to the Welsh Marches with instruction to hold the Lancastrian forces in Wales and his ally the Earl of Warwick was left in charge in London.

On 9th December 1460, Richard together with his second son Edmund, Earl of Rutland, and the Earl of Salisbury, marched his troops north to deal with them. However, as they arrived in Yorkshire they found he was outnumbered by the Lancastrian troops that had gathered when the Battle of Wakefield began. Although he occupied Sandal Castle, York

The entry of Princess Margaret into York, 1503.

sortied from this secure base on 30th December. The rationale for this move has been debated and might have been simple overconfidence or perhaps treachery by supposed allies.

The force raised by York and Salisbury was estimated to be maybe eight or nine thousand men, though some suggest it was far smaller than this. The expectation was to recruit local forces through a Commission of Array or a 'muster' i.e. a call to arms. After York himself, the Neville family was one of the wealthiest and most influential families in the North. Additionally, along with great estates, the Earl of Salisbury was Warden of the Eastern March. However, other powerful northern nobles, particularly the influential and often troublesome Percys, were rivals to York and Salisbury. Furthermore, the Nevilles were themselves divided with various factions largely disinherited and usurped by others. This was the complex and bitter political landscape in which the drama unfolded. York probably underestimated the Lancastrian numbers in their northern army which was still drawing in more troops. Early clashes did not bode well for Richard when, on 16th December, the Battle of Worksop took place in Nottinghamshire, York's vanguard engaging with the Duke of Somerset's West Country force as it moved north to join the other Lancastrian contingents; the Yorkist force was defeated.

It seems that the Yorkist army left Sandal Castle and marched down the present-day Manygates Lane toward where the Lancastrians were located to the north of the castle. However, as York met the Lancastrians in front of his troops, others attacked from both the flank and the rear. He was cut off from the castle so that in the words of chronicler Edward Hall (*Edward Hall's Chronicle*, c. 1500s): '... but when he was in the plain ground between his castle and the town of Wakefield, he was environed on every side, like a fish in a net, or a deer in a buckstall; so that he manfully fighting was within half an hour slain and dead, and his whole army discomfited.'

Some writers suggested that 2,500 Yorkists and 200 Lancastrians died though others gave figures of only 700 Yorkist fighters dead. Numbers in such conflicts are rarely accurate or reliable. Richard was killed during the battle or else captured and quickly executed. It was said that he was unhorsed and suffered a crippling knee wound, but nevertheless, that he and his closest followers fought to the death at that place. Other commentators claimed that he was captured by Sir James Luttrell of Devonshire, taunted by his captors and then beheaded.

York's second son, Edmund, Earl of Rutland, tried to flee across Wakefield Bridge, but overtaken, was killed; perhaps by Lord Clifford as revenge for his own father's death at the Battle of St Albans. Sir Thomas Neville, the Earl of Salisbury's second son was also killed during the conflict, and Salisbury's son-in-law William, Lord Harington, and his father William Bonville were both captured and executed. In many cases, this harsh treatment was a chance to settle feuds and old scores between families. Earl Salisbury escaped the battlefield only to be captured the following night. Sadly for Salisbury, while the nobles might have accepted a generous ransom for his life, his local commoners were not inclined to be kindly toward him. It seems that he was an oppressive lord and hearing of his downfall, they dragged him from Pontefract Castle and beheaded him.

The death of Richard of York did not end the war, or the claims of the House of York to the Crown. But after the Battle of Wakefield a rather grizzly episode in York's military history took place. The heads of the Duke of York, the Duke of Rutland, and the Earl of Salisbury were displayed over the south-western gate of York's city walls, Micklegate Bar. The former Duke of York, the short-lived King Richard, was sporting a paper crown with sign stating, 'Let York overlook the town of York'.

The result was devastating to the House of York, with Richard killed and his army wasted. Numerous leading Yorkist nobles and their relatives perished in the fighting and others were captured and executed. However, with Richard dead, his son, Edward of York, assumed the throne.

The White Rose

Symbolic of Yorkshire and synonymous with the House of York is the white heraldic rose, the White Rose of Yorkshire, Rose Alba or Rose Argent. This has been adopted as an emblem for Yorkshire itself and is said to have originated in the fourteenth century, with Edmund of Langley, the first Duke of York. Edmund founded the House of York as a cadet branch of the then royal House of Plantagenet. The white rose has symbolic connection to the Virgin Mary, known as the 'Mystical Rose of Heaven'; the white of the rose represents innocence, purity, joy and glory. Then, during the Wars of the Roses in the fifteenth century, the White Rose was the taken by Yorkist forces in opposition to their bitter rivals, the House of Lancaster. However, there is a twist since the red rose of Lancaster was a later, possibly Victorian, invention along with the name of the conflict as the Wars of the Roses; according to some it was better described as The Cousins' War. The red rose was not actually used by the Lancastrians at that time.

A white rose also emerged as a symbol during the late seventeenth century when the Jacobites adopted it as their emblem to celebrate White Rose Day on 10th June. This was the anniversary of the birth of King James III of England and VIII of Scotland in 1688. The White Rose of Scotland (also called the Scots Rose or Burnet Rose) was taken as a Scottish emblem from the time of Charles Edward Stuart (Bonnie Prince Charlie) in the 1700s, and is celebrated in poems and ballads.

In the military history of York and Yorkshire, the white rose holds a very special place. Not only the symbol of the royal House of York, it is also linked to Yorkshire soldiers and the origins of Yorkshire Day. After the Battle of Minden in Prussia on 1st August 1759, Yorkshiremen of the 51st Regiment, a predecessor of the King's Own Yorkshire Light Infantry, as a tribute to their fallen comrades, picked white roses from bushes close by the battlefield. The plucked blooms were placed in their coats and to commemorate the day, the fallen, and the act, Yorkshire Day is held on that date every year.

The Battles of Ferrybridge and of Towton

This bloody conflict continued as Richard Duke of York's son, having crushed the Lancastrians in battle as described below, claimed the throne as King Edward IV. He was briefly deposed in 1470 but won back the throne soon after.

Although the conflict dragged out over thirty years or more, the Wars of the Roses included only a few months of actual combat and fewer than twenty significant battles; though some were especially gory. The most gruesome of all, and one of the worst ever fought on English soil, was the Battle of Towton, and its preliminary engagement, the Battle of Ferrybridge, both in Yorkshire west of York.

The Battle of Ferrybridge on 28th March 1461 was a build-up to the Battle of Towton. Following his father's bloody death, Edward proclaimed himself King of England. So, as King Edward IV he gathered a large army and marched north to the Lancastrian stronghold beyond Yorkshire's River Aire. Then, on 27th March, the Earl of Warwick in charge of the York vanguard crossed the river at Ferrybridge. The bridge had been broken by the Lancastrians and so the Yorkists mended the gaps with planks. While undertaking this perilous crossing, Warwick lost many men to the freezing water and to cascades of arrows from the Lancastrians north of the river. However, once the waterway was crossed successfully, the Lancastrians were driven off, the bridge repaired, and Warwick and his troops established camp on the north bank.

The following dawn, the York vanguard was ambushed by a large Lancastrian troop commanded by Lord Clifford and John, Lord Neville, the latter being Warwick's cousin. Surprised and confused Warwick's small group took severe casualties and Lord FitzWalter, his second-in-command, was mortally wounded as he rallied the troops, dying a week later. Warwick's half-brother with the unfortunate title of 'The Bastard of Salisbury' was killed and while retreating, Warwick himself was injured by an arrow in the leg. It was suggested that around 3,000 men died at Ferrybridge.

However, following the battle, Edward himself arrived on the scene together with his main force and with Warwick they returned to the River Aire bridge which they found once more to be destroyed. Warwick sent his uncle, Lord Fauconberg, and the York cavalry upstream to cross via the ford at Castleford from where they set off in pursuit of Lord Clifford and his soldiers. In sight of the main Lancastrian army Fauconberg caught up with Lord Clifford and beat him in a furious struggle; Clifford was killed by an arrow to the throat after removing his protective armour for some unknown reason.

The Battle of Towton was fought on 29th March 1461, when the Yorkist forces of Edward IV met Margaret of Anjou's Lancastrians near the village of Towton located south-east of York, just south of Tadcaster. This horribly violent battle confirmed Edward, Duke of York, as King Edward IV (1461–83) in place of the troubled Lancastrian, Henry VI (1422–61). The battle has been said to be the largest and bloodiest battle ever on English soil though Boudicca's defeat to the Romans at the Battle of Watling Street runs it close. It is believed that around 50,000 troops took part, (though some estimates go as high as 80,000). Fighting for hours in the middle of a snowstorm on that bleak Palm Sunday, up to 28,000 men died on the battlefield.

Richard Duke of York claiming the throne in 1455 as King Richard II.

As the engagement began, Edward found himself considerably outnumbered since the troops of his ally the Duke of Norfolk were late in arriving. The conflict started with the mutual exchange of volleys of arrows before the armies closed to commence fierce hand-to-hand fighting. Although the Lancastrians had a strong topographical position on high ground, the inclement weather was an important factor. With snow blowing into their eyes the archers could not see their targets, and the wind was also against them. For the York archers the strong wind carried their arrows high and far, and they were also able to re-use the fallen arrows of the Lancastrian bowman that had fallen short. After about ten hours or so of unremitting combat, it was said that the nearby river ran red with blood. When the Duke of Norfolk arrived with fresh troops the battle finally turned in York's favour.

The ultimate outcome was a rout for the Yorkists and defeat for the Lancastrian cause, with Edward IV confirmed as the incumbent monarch ... for now at least. Apart from a brief period in 1470, he ruled a relatively stable county until his death in 1483.

The Closing Stages of the Wars of the Roses

Edward's death plunged the kingdom into further conflict and chaos, and gave York a man who was perhaps the most infamous or most unfairly maligned monarch in English history. It all depends on your point of view. During the period of the York–Lancaster conflict, there were five different monarchs and of these, three were killed or executed by their rivals. Following the deaths of his father and elder brother in battle, the young Richard of York, destined to become Richard III, was sent abroad for his safety. From the age of eight he lived in the Low Countries where he was relatively safe. Then, after Edward's climactic victory at Towton he came back to England to see his brother at last crowned as crowned as Edward IV. Richard then spent his formative teenage years living with his cousin, the Earl of Warwick, at Middleham Castle in the Yorkshire Dales. It was here that he would have been trained in his knightly skills and received the education fitting to his future role. But, as in such fickle times, Warwick defected to the Lancastrian cause and in 1470 both Richard and his brother Edward IV fled to Burgundy, with Warwick having reinstated Henry IV as king. Despite being only eighteen, Richard assumed importance in the ensuing conflict that brought Edward back to the throne. One result was that even at such an early age, Richard was a significant landowner with numerous titles and estates; and consequent on his role in restoring Edward as king, he became the Lieutenant of the North and Commander-in Chief against the Scots. With the Council of the North set up by Edward to administer governmental affairs, northern England was effectively under Richard's control from his base in York. Indeed, in the city where the council met and in the surrounding county of Yorkshire, Richard was immensely popular. (This was evidenced after his defeat and death at the hands of Henry Tudor, when many in York denied the Tudor legitimacy and stayed loyal to Richard.)

The Princes in the Tower

The key controversy surrounding Richard and his legitimacy as king and his humanity as a person, concerned his possible role in the disappearance of the 'Princes in the Tower' following Edward IV's death in April 1483. Edward was to be succeeded by his twelve-year old son Edward with Richard as Lord Protector of the realm. Richard provided a personal escort for the new king in waiting and his brother Richard as they journeyed from Ludlow to a safe residence in the Tower of London with a coronation planned to occur soon afterwards. However, before the young prince was crowned as King Edward V, his claim was declared invalid because Edward IV had been married previously and the prince was from his second and, it was asserted, illegitimate marriage. An assembly of Lords and commoners upheld this opinion, and within a day, Richard was himself crowned king as Richard III, the coronation on the 6th July. However, after August of that year, though supposedly lodged in safety at the Tower of London, the two young princes were never again seen in public. Many people held Richard accountable for their deaths.

York's most famous or perhaps infamous king, Richard III.

The Endgame of the Roses: The Battle of Bosworth

Richard's reign was not only controversial but it was also very short-lived. A combination of disaffected Yorkists, many being supporters of Edward IV, and the Lancastrian rump came together in opposition to the recently crowned monarch. The original intention was to restore Edward V to the throne, but it soon became clear that he was most likely dead already and they turned to the exiled Henry Tudor. Planned by the Duke of Buckingham and allies, the intention was to bring Henry and his supporters by ship from France to meet an army led by Buckingham. But when poor weather forced Henry to turn back, Buckingham's soldiers deserted; he was captured, convicted of treason, and on the 2nd November 1483, beheaded.

RICHARD III *Killed in* BOSWORTH-FIELD

Richard III at Bosworth Field.

The following August, having gathered together invasion army of Tudor loyalists and mercenaries in France, Henry set sail for his native Wales. From here he went north to recruit reinforcements at Shrewsbury and then headed east into England. Aware of the invading army Richard was occupied with garnering his own troops around Leicester, and on 20th August they set out to meet Tudor and cut off his route to London. Two days later the opposing forces met at Bosworth. While the true figures are not known exactly, it is clear from the outset that the king's forces outnumbered those of Tudor; perhaps 8,000 men versus five thousand. Henry Tudor made the more experienced Earl of Oxford his military commander and stayed well back in the rear with his personal bodyguard. The key turning point in the battle appears to be when Richard and a detachment of knights attempted to end it all by attacking Henry directly. In spite of getting close to the would-be king and his bodyguard, it is said to within a sword's length, and even killing his standard-bearer, Richard and his fighters were repelled. William Lord Stanley whose force was supposedly allied with Richard but not yet committed to the field, now decided to switch sides and the fate of the battle turned. It was said that Richard 'alone, was killed fighting manfully in the thickest press of his enemies'; struck repeatedly in the head he was killed.

The Lost King

York's most famous and for some most infamous monarch has still not totally left us or at least the public imagination. It was believed for many years that the body had been lost, cast into the River Soar. Richard was the last English king slain on the battlefield and after the conflict his naked body was put on public display prior to burial in Greyfriars Church, Leicester. From that time, the fate of the corpse became something of a mystery and the exact location, if it remained, was believed lost with the dissolution of the monasteries. However, a detailed and persistent search ensued during the early years of the twenty-first century and the location of the church and possible site of burial were found and a body discovered. Application of DNA, soil and dental analysis by Leicester University confirmed that this was the lost skeleton of Richard III, the last Plantagenet king of England. However, once the analysis of the skeleton and grave was over, the question remained of a site for the reburial of a monarch – something of a controversy.

A group of people known as the Plantagenet Alliance was established to represent fifteen individuals claiming descent from Richard III. The Alliance was passionate that the last resting place of Richard III should be his home city of York. Leicester, they argued, was the place of his undoing and therefore inappropriate. York City Council felt they had the moral high ground in the argument and Richard should indeed be returned to York. (It is hard not to feel that neither Leicester nor York were immune to the tourism potential of Richard's corpse more than 500 years after his death. As in many walks of life, dying has never been a barrier to stardom.) A legal debate followed with a judge ruling that opposing factions might legally contest the matter but urging them settle out of court. A subsequent ruling, however, decided that the courts could not interfere with the original choice of Leicester and so, in 2015, Richard III was reburied in Leicester Cathedral in a ceremony that included a poetry reading by Richard-descendant, actor Benedict Cumberbatch.

Richard III remains a hugely controversial figure, in part due to the pro-Tudor play-wright William Shakespeare. Whether or not he was guilty or responsible for the various crimes of which he was accused, it is hard to say. Certainly, recent historians have treated him less harshly though not exonerating him completely. Any actions must surely be considered in the context of the times, a ruthless age of private feuds, rival families and fiefdoms with claims on power and land, in which disputes were settled by bloody intim-idation and raw violence. Either way, Richard remains dear to many Yorkists and must be the city's most famous military leader.

The Pilgrimage of Grace

These were times of violence and dramatic swings in dominance and religious or political tolerance. The reign of another Tudor, Henry VIII, was no exception. While not strictly a military matter, the Pilgrimage of Grace, described as 'the most serious of all Tudor rebellions', was a hugely significant popular rising in Yorkshire during October 1536. The people rose against King Henry VIII's separation from the Roman Catholic Church, the Dissolution of the Monasteries, and many policies of the king's chief minister, Thomas Cromwell. There were other particular social, economic and political grievances with numerous risings and protests across northern England and farther south into Lincolnshire. The Lincolnshire uprising occurred twelve days prior to the Pilgrimage of Grace, a term now reserved for the Yorkshire uprising. This has often been presented as a 'spontaneous mass protest of the conservative elements in the North of England angry with the religious upheavals instigated by King Henry VIII' but clearly the commoners and lower gentry had other issues of concern including economic con-ditions. The rising grew following the brutal suppression of the Lincolnshire movement (which numbered 22,000 protesters) and began on 13th October 1536. One issue was to do with the Statute of Uses which was a complex mechanism that Henry was employing in order to resolve his own financial problems, and was deeply unpopular. Many northern people also objected to how Henry VIII had treated his wife, Catherine of Aragon, and her successor, Anne Boleyn, being unpopular as she was rumoured to be Protestant and was a southerner. However, her execution in 1536 on trumped-up charges of adultery and treason undermined Henry's reputation further. Additionally, those of aristocratic lineage disliked and feared Thomas Cromwell whom they considered 'base born' and highly dangerous. Finally, religion and church were at the core of people's concerns. For many northerners the local church was the centre of their community life and ordinary folk were deeply concerned about their church plate and other valuables or relics being confiscated. Rumours abounded about things like baptisms being taxed. For many in and around York who were deeply conservative by nature, the recently released 'Ten Articles' and the new order of prayer issued by the government in 1535 were of serious concern, and counter to the established beliefs of most northerners. This situation was a pow-der-keg of discontent and the worries of the Yorkshire people, from peasants to high aris-tocracy were to be more than confirmed by the dissolution of the Monasteries set in train between about 1536 and 1541.

In terms of the 'rising', the insurgents were led by Robert Aske, a barrister from London, resident of the Inns of Court, and youngest son of Sir Robert Aske of Aughton near Selby, south of York. Robert's family were from Aske Hall in Richmondshire, North Yorkshire. Aske led a throng of around 9,000 people who now entered and occupied York. He arranged for expelled monks and nuns to return to their religious houses and the newly installed tenants of the king were driven out. Catholic observances were resumed throughout the city and the region.

The authorities were both rattled and angered by this show of strength rather than the subservience that Henry generally demanded and expected. The 'Pilgrimage' was so successful that at Scawsby Leys, near Doncaster the representatives of the Crown, Thomas Howard, 3rd Duke of Norfolk, and George Talbot, 4th Earl of Shrewsbury, decided to negotiate with the protestors. By this point, Robert Aske had gathered around thirty to forty thousand people. Norfolk, on realizing the huge numbers set against him and the Earl of Shrewsbury (who had about 5,000 and 7,000 men respectively), feared a massacre. So they negotiated and gave assurances such as the promise of a general pardon and then of a Parliament to be held at York within a year. There was also to be a reprieve for the abbeys until this Parliament had met to discuss the matter. Rather foolishly, and certainly naively, Aske trusted the king's representatives and dismissed his followers, their objectives apparently achieved.

In fact, Henry VIII had not authorized Thomas Howard, 3rd Duke of Norfolk to grant any remedies for the people's grievances or to meet any of their demands. Furthermore, Norfolk's political enemies and rivals had been suggesting to Henry that the Howards could, if they really wanted, suppress such a rebellion of peasants quite easily: in other words, they said, Norfolk sympathized with the Pilgrims and the Rising.

Then, in February 1537, a new rising broke out in Cumberland and Westmorland. This was not authorized by Aske but was called Bigod's Rebellion, under Sir Francis Bigod, of Settrington in North Yorkshire. Knowing that the promises he had earlier made on behalf of the king were not going to be met, when the Pilgrims in the new uprising did not disperse as requested, Norfolk responded quickly and decisively. The rebellion failed with Bigod, Aske and several other rebels, such as Darcy, John Hussey, 1st Baron Hussey of Sleaford, the Chief Butler of England, Sir Thomas Percy and Sir Robert Constable, all arrested, convicted of treason and executed. So during 1537, Bigod was hanged at Tyburn, lords Darcy and Hussey were both beheaded, Thomas Moigne, MP for Lincoln was hanged, drawn and quartered, Sir Robert Constable was hanged in chains at Hull, and Robert Aske likewise at York.

Overall, 216 people were executed including several lords and knights (Sir Thomas Percy, Sir Stephen Hamerton, Sir William Lumley, Sir John Constable and Sir William Constable), six abbots (Adam Sedbar, Abbot of Jervaulx, William Trafford, Abbot of Sawley, Matthew Mackarel, Abbot of Barlings and Bishop of Chalcedon, William Thirsk, Abbot of Fountains and the Prior of Bridlington), thirty-eight monks, and sixteen parish priests. Sir Nicholas Tempest, Bowbearer of the Forest of Bowland, was hanged at Tyburn, and Sir John Bulmer was hanged, drawn and quartered (also at Tyburn), and his wife Margaret Stafford burnt at the stake at Smithfield. Additionally, late in 1538, Sir Edward Neville, Keeper of the Sewer, was beheaded. With the leaders arrested, the Duke of Norfolk had been able to suppress the rebellion and martial law was imposed across the troublesome regions such as Yorkshire.

The trial and execution of major leaders were recorded in *Wriothesley's Chronicle* as follows:

Also the 16 day of May [1537] there were arraigned at Westminster afore the King's Commissioners, the Lord Chancellor that day being the chief, these persons following: Sir Robert Constable, knight; Sir Thomas Percy, knight, and brother to the Earl of Northumberland; Sir John Bulmer, knight, and Ralph Bulmer, his son and heir; Sir Francis Bigod, knight; Margaret Cheney, after Lady Bulmer by untrue matrimony; George Lumley, esquire; Robert Aske, gentleman, that was captain in the insurrection of the Northern men; and one Hamerton, esquire, all which persons were indicted of high treason against the King, and that day condemned by a jury of knights and esquires for the same, whereupon they had sentence to be drawn, hanged and quartered, but Ralph Bulmer, the son of John Bulmer, was reprieved and had no sentence. And on the 25 day of May, being the Friday in Whitsun week, Sir John Bulmer, Sir Stephen Hamerton, knights, were hanged and headed; Nicholas Tempest, esquire; Doctor Cockerell, priest; Abbot quondam of Fountains; and Doctor Pickering, friar, were drawn from the Tower of London to Tyburn, and there hanged, bowelled and quartered, and their heads set on London Bridge and divers gates in London.

And the same day Margaret Cheney, 'other wife to Bulmer called', was drawn after them from the Tower of London into Smithfield, and there burned according to her judgment, God pardon her soul, being the Friday in Whitsun week; she was a very fair creature, and beautiful.

Despite being a focus for such problems, York remained a major religious and political centre through until the Stuart kings. Although the city suffered considerably during Henry VIII's English Reformation and the separation from Rome, the king did re-establish the Council of the North based in York to act as an advisory body and control-centre for northern England. This was set up under Henry's illegitimate son, the Duke of Richmond and met in the old Abbot's House of St Mary's. Its functions included acting as a regional court and administrative body; it assumed additional powers during the reigns of Elizabeth I and James I.

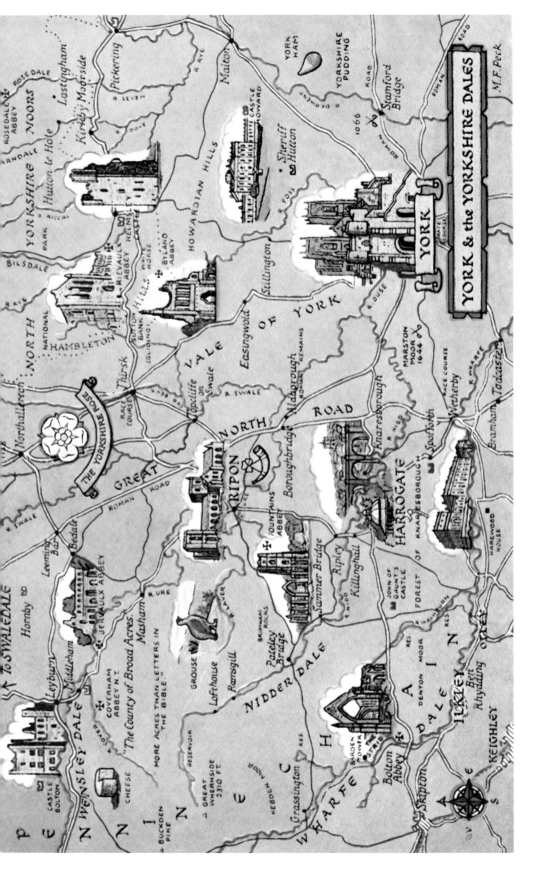

YORK & the YORKSHIRE DALES

M.F.Peck.

YORK

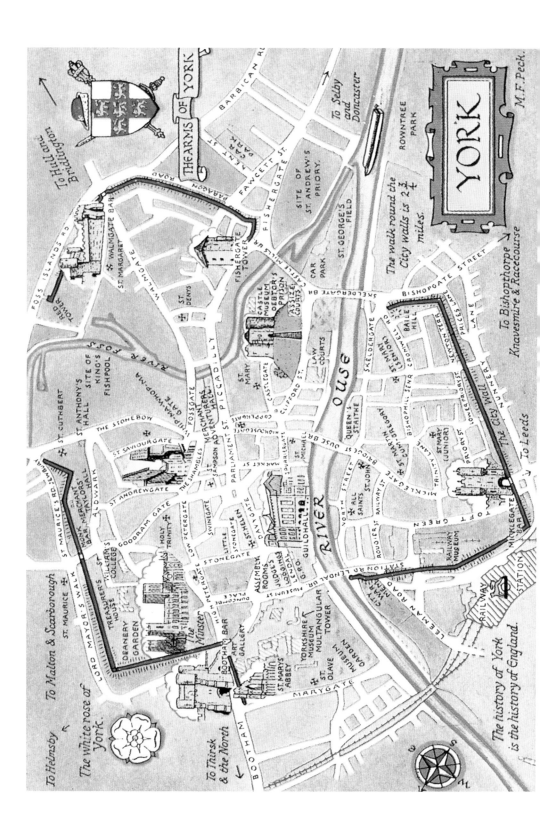

A Roman auxiliary.

ROYAL ARMS.

York historic Pageant. 1909.

ANGLO-SAXON SOLDIER, A.D. 1066.

An Anglo-Saxion warrior, *c.* 1066.

Yorkshire Regiment patrol in Afghanistan. (Photo Sgt Wes Calder RLC / MoD)

Medieval combat in the War of the Roses, a re-enactment. (Photo Paul Kitchener)

Yorkshire Regiment deployment by RAF Chinooks in Afghanistan. (Photo MoD)

ROYAL ARMS.

York Historic Pageant, 1909.

A soldier from the Stuart period, *c.* 1630.

Drummer from the first Yorkshire Regiment, early 1900s.

Yorkshire Regiment live-firing training. (Photo MoD)

Private in the East Yorkshire Regiment, early 1900s.

Crest of the Prince of Wales's Own Regiment of Yorkshire.

The RAF Swordfish, produced under licence by Blackburn Aircraft Company at their works at Sherburn-in-Elmet and Brough in Yorkshire, entered service in 1934 and amazingly served throughout the Second World War, the last biplane to do so. (Photo MoD)

THE YORK & LANCASTER REGIMENT

Cap Badge. 1865
65th Foot

Medal of Merit. 1806
84th Foot

Crest of the York and Lancaster Regiment.　　The Princess Royal's Dragoon Guards.

100 Squadron RAF Hawk above the clouds over Yorkshire. (Photo MoD)

Sergeant Major, Yorkshire Regiment, early 1900s.

The Victoria Cross.

4 Mechanized Brigade on desert mobility training, in Jackal 2 vehicles. (Photo MoD)

6. THE ENGLISH CIVIL WAR

Over time however, worse was to follow, since during the English Civil War, as a Royalist stronghold, York, was besieged for long periods. The English Civil War ran from 1642 to 1651 and became a bitter and bloody struggle between Parliament on the one hand and monarchy on the other. However, it does always seem slightly strange to call this *the* English Civil War when clearly from the earlier chapters there was at times almost continual warring across the country. However, this cataclysmic affair triggered new skirmishes, battles and political in-fighting between Parliamentarians (or 'Roundheads' as they became known) and Royalists (or 'Cavaliers'). At the core of the dispute were the manner of England's government, matters of religious tolerance, and of course, the roles

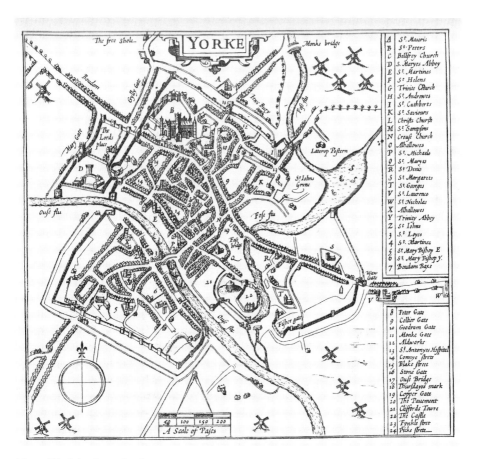

Map of York in the early 1600s.

of the monarch himself. There were two principal wars, the first (1642–46) and the second (1648–49) which saw King Charles I (1600–49) and his allies versus the Long Parliament and its supporters. The third war was from 1649 to 1651 and between the future King Charles II and his allies, against the so-called Rump Parliament, this third phase closing with the Parliamentarian victory at the Battle of Worcester on 3rd September 1651.

The war triggered three main outcomes: 1) the trial and execution of Charles I in 1649, 2) the exile of Charles's son in 1651 and 3) replacement of English monarchy. Originally the Crown was displaced by the Commonwealth of England (1649–53) which in turn gave way to the Protectorate rule of Oliver Cromwell (1653–58) and then his son (1658–59). There were religious changes too, and in the long term, the role of the monarchy ruling under Parliamentary approval was established.

Charles I came to the throne in 1625 but was constantly at loggerheads with Parliament over money and royal prerogatives. York's importance had grown steadily during the reigns of Elizabeth and then Charles's father, James I, but Parliament abolished the Council of the North in 1641. However, during a period of the Civil War, Charles I made York his capital, establishing his court at the Abbot's House, now renamed King's Manor, and setting up a Royal mint close by.

The Siege of York

Following the outbreak of hostilities, in 1643, Royalist forces triumphed at the Battle of Adwalton Moor near Bradford and so gained control over much of Yorkshire. Parliamentary forces moved north under the command of Sir Thomas Fairfax and during summer 1644, established a siege of York which was defended by the Marquess of Newcastle.

During March and early April of 1643, the marquess had undertaken a number of actions intended to delay or prevent the Scottish Covenanters (sympathetic to the Parliamentarian Puritans) from crossing the River Tyne and surrounding the city of Newcastle upon Tyne. However, a Roundhead cavalry force, commanded by Sir Thomas Fairfax, crossed the Pennines and entered West Yorkshire from Lancashire. In order to stop Sir Thomas meeting his father, Lord Fairfax, in Kingston upon Hull, Royalist forces occupied the town of Selby south of York. Nevertheless, Sir Thomas's army with infantry reinforcements brought by Sir John Meldrum took Selby and captured the Royalist leaders there.

When the marquess got the news of this turn of events he realized that York itself was under threat. The loss of the city of York as the principal centre of Royalist power in northern England would be a catastrophic blow to the cause, and he hastily left Newcastle in order to head off an assault by the Fairfaxes. The Scots leader, Lord Leven, left a force under the Earl of Callendar to hold the Royalist garrison at Newcastle and with his main army headed south in the wake of the marquess. By 22nd April, the Parliamentarians and the Covenanters joined forces at Wetherby, around fourteen miles west of York, and moved eastward to lay siege to the city.

The early stages of the siege of York involved a relatively loose blockade with the allies intent on taking the smaller Royalist garrisons around the city and which

The siege of York in 1644.

controlled communications with the Parliamentarian forces based at Hull. However, on 3rd June, reinforcements arrived in the shape of the Parliamentarian Army of the Eastern Association commanded by the Earl of Manchester, and York was now completely encircled. The siege began in earnest with Lord Leven now commander-in-chief of the combined armies, in Parliament described as the 'Army of Both Kingdoms'. This was an astute move designed to bolster the Scottish Covenanters in the north where the Royalists were traditionally strong and the Parliamentarians weak. Additionally, Lord Leven was an experienced and highly respected soldier and already a veteran of the Thirty Years' War.

The Relief of York

King Charles's cousin and military commander, Prince Rupert of the Rhine, was one of the outstanding military leaders of the war. News of the siege of York had quickly reached Oxford, which King Charles had now established as his wartime capital. From 24th April to 5th May, a council of war took place that was attended by his advisers including, of course, Prince Rupert. The decision was that while Charles played for time in Oxford, Rupert would set out with an army to relieve York. Rupert gathered a force and marched through north-west England, attracting reinforcements and further recruits on the way. They struck across the Pennine hills and down to the plain of York to relieve the city. Rupert arrived at the head of an army believed to have numbered around 15,000 men and which broke the Parliamentarian siege.

The Roundheads' Forced Retreat from York

Clearly aware of Prince Rupert's force drawing near, the allies were hoping for reinforcements from the English Midlands led by Sir John Meldrum and the Earl of Denbigh. However, when it was realized that these forces would not arrive in time, and with their own armies in the York area cut off by the city's rivers and thus vulnerable to piecemeal attack, they decided to abandon the siege on the night of 30th June. The Allied armies moved to the village of Hessay prior to assembling on Marston Moor. Here they blocked Rupert's expected direct route to York that followed the old Roman road of Ermine Street or today's modern A59. Furthermore, from this strategic position they could, if needed, move south to stop Rupert's army cutting through via Wetherby.

By the time he arrived at York, Rupert was unsure of how best to proceed, and earlier news from Oxford had probably compounded his doubts. The following message arrived from Charles:

> But now I must give the true state of my affairs, which, if their condition be such as enforces me to give you more peremptory commands than I would willingly do, you must not take it ill. If York be lost I shall esteem my crown little less; unless supported by your sudden march to me; and a miraculous conquest in the South, before the effects of the Northern power can be found here. But if York be relieved, and you beat the rebels' army of both kingdoms, which are before it, then (but otherwise not) I may possibly make a shift upon the defensive to spin out time until you come to assist me. Wherefore I command and conjure you, by the duty and affection that I know you bear me, that all new enterprises laid aside, you immediately march according to your first intention, with all your force to the relief of York. But if that be either lost, or have freed themselves from the besiegers, or that for want of powder, you cannot undertake that work, that you immediately march with your whole strength, directly to Worcester to assist me and my army; without which, or you having relieved York by beating the Scots, all the successes you can afterwards have must infallibly be useless onto me.

Prince Rupert took the message from Charles as a command to relieve York *and* defeat the allied army *and* then head south to support the king at Oxford. When he had set out from Liverpool to Preston, Rupert's army was around 14,000 strong and the Preston surrendered without resistance. He had gone via Clitheroe, crossing the Pennines to Skipton and halted there for three days from 26th June to 28th June to carry out essential maintenance and allow reinforcements from Cumberland and Westmoreland to arrive. He reached the Royalist garrison at Knaresborough Castle on 30th June, and was now fourteen miles north-west of York.

As the Parliamentarians had withdrawn from the siege, some of Rupert's cavalry were able to reach York and make contact with the city's garrison. So with York relieved for now, the Marquess of Newcastle sent Rupert a message of welcome and congratulations. Rupert's response was an order for the incumbent forces to march from the city to meet him and join battle with the allies. It appears that troops in York hesitated leaving and some were unwilling to fight until they were paid monies owing to them.

The Battle of Marston Moor

Nevertheless, at about midday, Rupert was joined on Marston Moor by the Marquess of Newcastle and a mounted troop of 'gentleman volunteers'. The Prince greeted them with, 'My Lord, I wish you had come sooner with your forces, but I hope we shall yet have a glorious day.' Newcastle wanted to await an expected force of 3,000 under Colonel Clavering and another 2,000 from garrisons gathered en route before joining battle. However, armed with his letter from the king, Rupert was determined to engage and defeat the enemy immediately. He also hoped that catching the enemy unawares might help counter-balance the Royalists' numerical inferiority. Yet in the absence of Newcastle's infantry, and with his own infantry exhausted from a long march, Rupert was forced to wait and rest. Nevertheless, the odds against the Royalists grew as time passed with Scots and Parliamentarian infantry and artillery returning from an aborted move southward.

So, early on 1st July, Royalist cavalry advanced from Knaresborough Castle and on to the moor as the allies prepared for battle. However, by now, Rupert had undertaken a twenty-two-mile flanking movement to the north-east with his main force to cross the River Ure at Boroughbridge and the River Swale at Thornton Bridge. It is these two rivers

Above left: Charles I.

Above right: Sir Thomas Fairfax.

The quadrangle of the ancient palace of the Stuart kings.

that merge to become the River Ouse which flows down to York. Rupert placed his troops behind this defensive feature, at the same time defeating the dragoons of the Earl of Manchester guarding a bridge of boats constructed across the Ouse at Poppleton just a few miles north of York. As the only crossing available to the allies above York, and with the only other crossing another bridge of boats at Acaster Malbis five miles south of the city, its loss effectively prevented allied troops crossing the river to engage the Royalists.

However, this was merely the beginning as the two armies of Rupert and of Fairfax came together; this was to be one of the largest battles of the entire civil war and one of the biggest battles on English soil. The Battle of Marston Moor was fought on 2nd July 1644 with a combined force of English Parliamentarians under Lord Fairfax and the Earl of Manchester, and the Scottish Covenanters under the Earl of Leven, defeating the Cavaliers under Prince Rupert and the Marquess of Newcastle. The result was a crushing defeat for the Royalists who had been heavily outnumbered and whose leaders actively distrusted and disliked one another. The siege of York was renewed and the city capitulated on 15th July 1644. In the subsequent pillaging and looting there was much damage done with many important buildings destroyed. Fairfax, as a native of Yorkshire, personally intervened in order to limit damage to York's churches, especially the Minster.

The casualties at Marston Moor were considerable and, as always, are difficult to account for with any precision. The battle proper had commenced at about 7 p.m. and around two hours later it was nearly fully dark but with a full moon rising. The countryside for miles around York was strewn with hundreds of dead soldiers, with confused fugitives from both sides wandering aimlessly. With the two armies numbering around 18,000 Royalists and 28,000 allies, there were probably about 4,000 Royalist soldiers killed, many of whom being in the final brave stand of Newcastle's 'whitecoats'. With about 1,500 men captured, the Royalist army lost all its guns plus hundreds of other weapons. The allies recorded that only 300 of their soldiers were killed though this seems unduly optimistic bearing in mind the ferocious combat. One officer mortally wounded was Sir Thomas Fairfax's own brother, Charles, and another was Oliver Cromwell's nephew, Valentine Walton. The latter was struck by a cannonball early in the battle. Prince Rupert's right wing and reserve were routed by a combination of Cromwell's cavalry and the Covenanters' infantrymen, and he himself only avoided capture by hiding in a nearby bean field. For Rupert this was a disaster from which he never fully recovered.

Late into the night, Royalist generals and the stragglers made the short journey back to the sanctuary of York. Sir Thomas Glemham, the Governor of York, only allowed in those who were part of the garrison or in other words those few officers who had volunteered to take part in the action. He was worried that Parliamentarian cavalry might enter York

The King's Manor, York, from the Stuart period.

Above left: Rupert of the Rhine.

Above right: Roundhead soldier.

with or close behind the fugitive Royalists. As it was, the streets leading to Micklegate Bar, the western gate into York, were crammed full of wounded and fugitive soldiers.

The Marquess of Newcastle, his forces broken, defeated and slaughtered, and having spent his fortune in supporting the Royalist cause decided to leave to avoid, in his words, 'laughter of the court'. He departed for Scarborough just a day after the battle (3rd July) and sailed to exile in Hamburg, with many of his senior officers. For Rupert, in particular, this was a bitter blow as Marston Moor was the first time he had been decisively beaten. Deeply affected by the defeat he kept the king's letter close to him for the rest of his life. During the battle, he also lost his faithful dog Boye, his constant companion throughout his campaigns; this was celebrated in Parliamentarian propaganda after the battle. Two days following the defeat, Rupert gathered together around 5,000 cavalry and just a few hundred infantrymen mounted on spare horses and left York via Monk Bar i.e. on the north-eastern side in order to detour round Richmond to avoid interception, and thus recross the Pennines and back into Lancashire. From there he headed back south to join up with King Charles.

So, with the exile of Newcastle and the escape of Prince Rupert, with the exception of isolated garrisons, the Royalists in effect forsook northern England. Any remaining Royalist pockets were slowly neutralized, one by one, over the subsequent months. One Royalist cavalry detachment from the northern counties, the Northern Horse', continued to fight under Lord Digby and Sir Marmaduke Langdale but when they relieved a Royalist garrison at Pontefract Castle in West Yorkshire in February 1645, their undisciplined and licentious behaviour was so bad that former supporters of the Crown were swayed from the Royalist cause. The Northern Horse then attacked and initially defeated a Parliamentarian garrison based in the village of Sherburn-in-Elmet, south-east of York, protecting one of the routes into the city. However, the victory was short-lived as a second Parliamentarian troop led by Colonel Copley counter-attacked and routed the Royalists. This engagement in October 1645 was the end of the last significant Royalist force in northern England.

The strategic importance of York as the primary northern stronghold of the Royalists thus ended. York eventually recovered its position and influence. By 1660, it was the third-largest city in England after London and Norwich. York has always demonstrated a remarkable ability to bounce back from adversity.

Civil War re-enactment. (Photo Barry Skeates)

7. THE JACOBITE REBELLION

In terms of direct involvement, the Jacobite rebellions must count as 'nearly' events in York's history. There were two Jacobite uprisings, the first in 1715 to support the 'Old Pretender', James Francis Edward Stuart, the son of the deposed James II, and the second, and more significant event in 1745, led by the 'Young Pretender', the grandson of James II, to put his father on throne. The intention was to return the Stuarts to the English and Scottish monarchy and it has long been assumed that these seismic events mostly passed York by. That may have been the case after the first rebellion in 1715 when York's only major role was to house some of the prominent rebels in the secure walls of its castle dungeons. The first rebellion had been successful in northern Scotland but was halted at key places such as Stirling and Edinburgh. Once things turned against them, the rebels largely dissipated. A rebellion in west England was thwarted by prompt government action, but a similar uprising in Northumbria had more success as rebels joined with Scottish Jacobites crossing the border.

From here, they traversed northern England and pressed on down the western side of the country toward Preston in Lancashire. With 4,000 troops the rebels took Preston in November 1715 as the government soldiers retreated to Wigan. However, General Charles

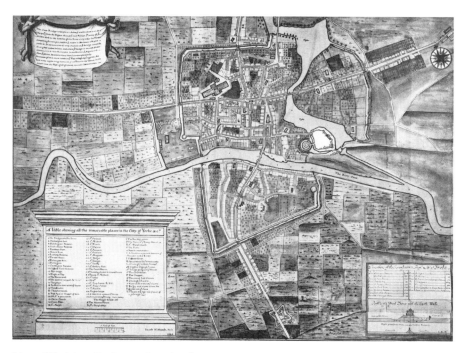

Map of York in 1685, by Jacob Richards.

Wills was directed to march north from Manchester to halt the Jacobite advance and with him were six regiments of regular soldiers. After a short siege rather than a pitched battle, Preston was taken and the rebellion effectively quashed. At the surrender, 1,468 Jacobites were taken prisoner, 463 of whom were English. Because the rebels had gone down the western flank of the Pennines, the impact on York was limited; if they had chosen an eastern route then the situation and indeed the outcome might have been very different. A number of senior rebels were held in the Tower of London and then executed, and others were held at York. Many were pardoned.

Interestingly, the Battle of Preston is sometimes claimed as the last 'battle' fought on English soil, but this rather depends on your definition of 'battle', and there are different interpretations. Other later conflicts are also contenders, such as a skirmish on Clifton Moor near Penrith in Cumbria on 18th December 1745 during the second Jacobite uprising, or even the rather odd Battle of Bossenden Wood at Hernhill in Kent on 31st May 1838 that was led by a former inmate of a lunatic asylum. Other industrial, social and political conflicts that were violently suppressed by the authorities also spring to mind, the Peterloo Massacre in St Peter's Field, Manchester on 16th August 1819 being one example. Either way, in this particular case, York remained relatively unaffected and unscathed by the Jacobites. Furthermore, it has been assumed by many historians that the same applied to the 1745 rebellion.

However, the impact of the second uprising, 'the '45', was re-examined by Jonathan Oates at the University of York in 2005, and this placed a new interpretation on the events. When the Young Pretender, Bonnie Prince Charlie, tried to seize the throne for his father some thirty years after the first rather abortive uprising that had been speedily suppressed, there was a somewhat mixed reaction within York. The north of England and especially some of

Layerthorpe Postern and Towers from the River Foss, by J. Halfpenny, 1807.

The Highland charge

The Highland charge, one of the most frightening examples of organized hand-to-hand combat, was developed as a battlefield shock tactic used by the Scottish Highland clans and evolved from their earlier methods but to include the use of firearms. Before the seventeenth century, Highlanders fought in close formations, led by their heavily armed warrior elite carrying battle axes or claymores (two-handed broadswords – from Gaelic *claidheamh mòr* or 'great sword'). However, as musket and cannon became more commonly used these tight formations were increasingly vulnerable. To deal with this, the seventeenth-century Highlanders evolved a lighter, one-handed, broadsword that was basket-hilted to protect the hand and used with a shield or *targe* strapped to the weaker arm and in the other hand, a dirk or biotag, 'long knife'. Armed with these weapons the Highlanders used the charge which in style was similar to older Celtic approaches to fighting as one side rushed at the other and attempted to break through the line of battle.

To execute the charge effectively necessitated remarkable bravery and commitment. Rushing headlong into musket range, the front ranks stood to suffer significant losses from at least one volley of shot. In this context, speed was at the core of the charge, with the Highlanders needing to cover the ground quickly to close with the enemy. Because of this, they preferred to charge downhill and over firm ground. Clothing was removed from the lower body to ease the speed of running and not to hinder them. The warriors ran forwards in units of a dozen or so, generally of kinsmen, and the units together formed a greater wedge-shaped battle-group. Once the Highlanders were in effective musket range of about sixty yards, the ones carrying firearms paused and together opened fire. The cloud of gunsmoke resulting from the coordinated discharge helped hinder the opposition's aim, and at the same time, the Highlanders dropped to the floor for additional protection from the enemy's return volley. Now was the final thrust of the Highland charge and with firearms dropped and sharp weapons drawn, the warriors made the ultimate rush onto the opposition lines. Shouting and crying out in Gaelic they endeavoured to get within striking distance taking their opponent's sword or bayonet on the shield and at the same time lunging in close and low down in order to thrust upwards into an enemy's torso.

Being on the receiving end of the charge was an unnerving experience and for infantrymen armed with muskets and bayonets, there was a delay in lowering the firearm in order to fix the bayonet. That delay might prove fatal.

the powerful landowning families had long been of Catholic leanings and thus sympathetic to some aspects of the Stuart claim. However, overall the city remained anti-Jacobite. In the Minster, the Archbishop of York preached a sermon against the rebels, and in the city, a

Micklegate around 1800.

group of volunteers called the Yorkshire Association was convened in order to defend York against the Stuart forces should the need arise. This body included the mayor, the clerk and numerous men from the local gentry. Additional preparations included work to patch up the city walls. As in many towns and cities across England, the fear was not merely of attack by the rebels outside, but a concern about Catholic and other sympathizers within. In practice, in York itself the Protestants and Catholics had more or less lived in harmony for many decades with a reasonable degree of tolerance. With a threat of rebellion however, this situation might easily change. In the event, the final and decisive battle took place many miles to the north at Culloden in the Highlands of Scotland in 1746. In England, this triggered a corporate sigh of relief, in much of Scotland, despair as punitive suppression took place. When the Jacobite rebels were defeated, York sent congratulations to the king and furthermore, invited the successful commander, the Duke of Cumberland (known in Scotland as 'The Butcher'), to accept the freedom of the city presented in a hundred-guinea gold box.

The 1745 rebellion was a complex affair and in England potentially pitched the government of the day, the Whigs, against the Tories who had or were suspected of having sympathy for the Jacobite cause and for increased tolerance of Catholicism. So across both England and Scotland there was widespread suspicion over a wide spectrum of society.

Having arrived in Scotland in July 1745, Charles Stuart and his allies had raised a small army of Highlanders and marched southward. Edinburgh and other towns were soon been taken or else surrendered. Momentum was building and as the Jacobites headed southeast into lowland Scotland, the only significant opposition from government troops was

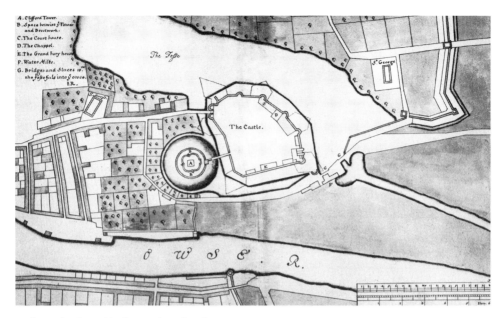

York Castle plan, 1685, by Jacob Richards.

at Prestonpans on 21st September where the British army was comprehensively routed. This event, which became part of Jacobite mythology, boosted the cause and left the north of England vulnerable to a major incursion. Indeed, by December 1745, the rebels reached Derby in the English Midlands. However, fed misinformation about a major Hanoverian army blocking their path to London, the Jacobites hesitated and headed back to Scotland and ultimately defeat at Culloden. From a York perspective, as it turned out, the invasion had again headed west and then south, thus missing the city. Nevertheless, with northern England exposed and largely undefended following Prestonpans, the people of York were for a while gripped with fear and apprehension about an imminent attack.

A key moment which put York on the map in terms of the '45 was a speech by the recently appointed Archbishop of York, Thomas Herring, and who was described at the time, as 'the last warrior bishop of England'. Acting with three Lord Lieutenants of Yorkshire, Herring was raising money to fund troops to defend York and the county of Yorkshire against invasion. An audience of 813 people had come from across the county to hear the speech said to be short but effective and to the point. The Archbishop stated that the Pretender was in Scotland, that Edinburgh had fallen, and Sir John Coe and the British army had been heavily defeated at Prestonpans. The rebels threatened invasion and the city and the county had to make the best provision they could against the enemy who, Herring asserted, were aided by 'our savage and bloodthirsty enemies', France and Spain. Furthermore, if their plan was successful, the result 'under these two Tyrannical and corrupted Crowns', would be 'Popery and Arbitrary Power'. King George II's reign was described as a blessing, and a 'mild Administration of a Just and Protestant King' threatened by the Jacobites who were aided

78

Above: Bishopthorpe Palace, York, the residence of his Grace the Archbishop of York, mid-1900s.

Right: James Edward Stuart, the Old Pretender.

The Suppression of Catholics

Persecution of Catholics by Protestants and vice versa, was a major issue during the reigns of Henry VIII and then Mary Tudor and Elizabeth I. In many cases, the results were brutal persecution and unmitigated violence. In this context, as a northern city with Catholic sympathies, York and its civic leaders were under a significant degree of suspicion.

In 1586, for example, Margaret Clitherow was arrested and called before the York Assizes accused of harbouring Roman Catholic priests. Margaret refused to plead which avoided a trial during which her children would have been tortured in order to extract the necessary incriminating information. Despite being pregnant with her fourth child, Clitherow, who was married to John Clitherow, a wealthy butcher and a chamberlain of the city, was executed on Lady Day, 1586. This horrendous incident took place in the Toll Booth at Ouse Bridge, and was by being crushed to death, a standard way of encouraging the accused to make a plea. She had converted to Catholicism in 1574, just three years after her marriage to her Anglican husband. However, his brother William was a Roman Catholic priest and so John Clitherow was sympathetic and on previous occasions had paid her fines for not attending Anglican services. In fact, Margaret was imprisoned in 1577 for failing to attend services and then twice more, all in York Castle; her third child was born in prison.

The grim task was allotted to two sergeants but they paid four desperate beggars to do the deed instead. Clitherow was stripped naked with a handkerchief tied over her face. She was then laid onto a sharp rock the size of a man's fist and the door from her own house was placed on top of her body. This door was then piled with rocks and stones until the sharp rock broke her back, death taking about fifteen minutes. The body was left there for six hours before the immense weight was removed. The ordeal triggered an outcry of revulsion even in those times of easy brutality. Queen Elizabeth I wrote to the citizens of York to express her own horror at the treatment of a woman, who, because of her sex, she said, should not have been executed.

by Spain and France. Herring went on to explain that Yorkshire as a wealthy county should take the lead and be prepared to pay for its defence. He also instructed clergymen present to educate and animate the people across the city and throughout the county. The speech ended with a call to unite to 'stop this dangerous Mischief'.

Herring was widely applauded and the Duke of Newcastle said to him, that 'He [George II] is very sensible how greatly your Grace's example and influence have contributed to encourage and promote that spirit of Loyalty which appears so universally among His faithful subjects in the County of Yorkshire'. (Herring later went on to become Archbishop of Canterbury from 1747 to 1757, perhaps reward for his staunch service.)

Meanwhile in York, the Archbishop's main role following the speech was to remain in York and help calm the fears of the populace with regard to any forthcoming attack. Although he did send his family away from the official residence at Bishopsthorpe, he himself stayed in the city, having had what he described as a sort of 'remonstrance from the city here that it will create some sort of uneasiness ... I will not stir'.

Catholicism & A History of Persecution

The Anglican Church was a vigorous supporter of the status quo in politics and religion, and York was a major ecclesiastical centre. Church bells were rung on days of religious or royal significance – and York had a lot of churches. Taking Herring's example, other clergymen preached from the pulpit against the rebels and the uprising. However, the Corporation of York was dominated by Tories and their motives and loyalties were suspect. So when they refused to have the homes of Catholics searched for military-type weapons or horses above a certain value, others took the lead. Guards were placed at the doors of premises and twenty-six horses were confiscated for the use of the army. In December 1745, the Convent and Catholic girls' school situated just outside Micklegate Bar was attacked by the mob and all its windows broken. It was known that in York there were around 220 practising Catholics, only a tiny proportion of the city's population. However, the persecution of Catholics over previous centuries indicated the potential hostility and intolerance.

The Margaret Clitherow incident serves as a grim reminder of attitudes and violence toward Catholics in the city at this time with fears of Papish plots and intrigues. For example, on 10th October 1745, it was reported that papists particularly in York itself, 'had rejoicings in ye private houses upon ye unfortunate affair of cope [the rout of the loyalist forces at Prestonpans]'. There was even a fear of an imminent uprising.

By October 1645, suspected Catholics, possible priests, and some Tories were being apprehended and brought to York for incarceration in the Castle. Some of the accused were soon released but many were held until March 1746, others as late as March 1747. The Duke of Norfolk was involved in securing releases and consequently his political enemies accused him of being a 'bigotted papist'. Propaganda and publicity spread fear and panic among the population with Jacobite rebels described as wild barbarians from the Scottish Highlands who would

The King's Manor in the 1800s.

plunder, murder, pillage and rape. As news of the Prestonpans defeat and imminent invasion reached York, many citizens began to plan exits to safer places. Some people departed south for London, and others at least sent their females away, citizens expecting the Scots to arrive very soon. Despite this, life went on and York was described as 'extremely full of noise and people', with things seemingly more under control by October 1745.

However, in November, the situation worsened and widespread panic ensued. On 20th November the rebels began their march south from Carlisle and by 22nd to the 24th November, on the streets of York it was believed the Jacobites might cross the Pennines and head eastward to the city. Families packed necessary belongings and set off for Scarborough, Burlington (i.e. Bridlington) and Hull. Others prepared boats on the river, ready to leave at short notice if necessary. A commentator noted that, 'it is not to be conceived how frightful the hurry was in the city of York this Wednesday, while the apprehension was strong that they would take this road. They are a little quieted today by the hopes that they are turned toward Lancashire ... if they come this way, not a soul will stay in York that can move'. By 24th November, the panic had subsided as it was clear that the rebels had taken the western route away from York, south through Lancashire. However, concerns returned in December when the Jacobite army retreating north from Derby, reached Rochdale, only forty miles from York. Rumours abounded and uncertainty remained throughout December.

Displayed Upon Micklegate Bar

York, as with London, had a long tradition of displaying heads and other body-parts of traitors and the vanquished on spikes along Micklegate Bar or other bars if Micklegate was overly full. One famous incident followed the execution of twenty-two Jacobite rebels, supporters of the exiled Stuart dynasty.

At the time the standard punishment for treason for men was to be hanged, drawn and quartered. Women were burnt at the stake, supposedly for the sake of decency. However, for males, the process often involved being dragged by a horse to the site of the gallows, being hanged in the normal way but without the drop to prevent the neck being broken and thereby delaying death, then finally being cut down from the rope to be disembowelled and further mutilated.

Following this gruesome public display, the heads of executed Jacobites were sent on a tour of the country. However, York was allowed to keep two and these were placed on display in the time-honoured fashion where they were left to gradually rot in public view. One twist of this fate was that most people believed that to go to Heaven a person had to be buried with their skull and at least two large bones. In this case, not only were the severed heads a warning to the people about insurrection but also a threat of eternal damnation.

Across Yorkshire, the county raised forty-one companies of volunteer infantry soldiers led by county lieutenants, and to fund this the county and city raised around £32,000. Fear of invasion remained alongside distrust of those within the city walls. Indeed, correspondence between the Jacobite Duke of Perth and the Old Pretender, James, suggested significant support for the Stuart cause in York, and that the county might raise a troop of 10,000 or more Jacobite supporters with the same from adjacent counties. However, it is hard to discern how much of this was mere fantasy and what carried real weight. Both Whigs and Tories were playing out dangerous political games and it was in the interests of the Whigs to cast doubt upon their Tory rivals. Whig Sir Rowland Winn suggested that there was 'good reason to believe that ye mayor and aldermen of ye City of York will not do their duty therein'. Nevertheless, it seems that most of the actions of the Corporation were distinctly loyalist in nature, for example, establishing a subscription to help fund the volunteer military force.

The Royal Dragoon Guards.

The next steps of preparation involved not only recruiting, assembling and training the soldiers, but also the troublesome task of arming them. After decades of peace, weapons were not easily available. Micklegate Ward provided 129 guns, 114 bayonets, and 83 swords. Adjoining parishes gave 131 guns and 94 bayonets. These weapons needed to be cleaned and put into good order for use. Ammunition was needed and casks of gunpowder ordered. Six weeks passed since the establishment of the troop and the Jacobites were massing just over the border in Scotland yet the soldiers were still not adequately equipped or prepared. A hundred more muskets were ordered from a dealer in Birmingham, and sixty muskets found to be unsuited to use by the soldiers were exchanged for twelve blunderbusses from the same dealer.

The troops also had to be clothed – captains having an allowance of £8 and privates outfitted in coats, breeches, hats, and cockades costing about eighteen shillings per man. The necessary cloth was in short supply and the full uniforms not available until early October. The regular infantry of the British army wore red jackets but the volunteers had blue jackets faced with red like the Royal Artillery. It seems officers gave their services free, sergeants were paid two shillings a day, corporals and drummers eighteen pence, and privates a shilling, about double that of regulars. Each company had a captain, two junior officers, three sergeants, two corporals, two drummers and probably around eighteen privates.

On the 5th November, to commemorate the demise of the Gunpowder Plot there was festivity with free beer for the volunteers. Then, by January 1746, the men were considered 'all well trained and disciplined' and there was a big celebration costing around £24 with bonfires and free ale for the men. Not everything went smoothly and criticism of the Corporation still lingered – especially over delays in equipping the troops. Testing some of the guns resulted in one exploding – hardly a testament to their readiness. Also, guns ordered from Birmingham had been commandeered by the Corporation for safe keeping lest they fall into enemy hands as the result of an assault. It still seemed the volunteers would not be able to adequately defend York in the event of an attack. Archbishop Herring expressed serious concern at the preparations stating that 'the attempts of a militia or new raised forces to preserve these towns are arrant folly'. Even so, despite the defeat of government forces at Falkirk in January, it was believed that, 'the Rebells are far distant from this City, the Town quiet, no appearance of Tumults or Disorders & therefore no occasion to keep Guards in Thursday market at the Barrs'.

Subscription monies were running low and York was manned by 150 regulars and 200 men of the independent city companies in order to deal with disorder or other problems. To all intents and purposes, with the imminent threat receding, the militia was disbanded and the men kept in arms now only one day per week. Therefore, on 27th January 1746, the troops were assembled, thanked for their services and weapons handed in. So ended York's final call to arms on home turf.

By the time of the '45, despite being a walled city it was considered by many that York was not really capable of being defended in the event of a siege. Expert opinion was that the defences might hold for an hour or so but no more, with three miles of wall described as 'ruinous' and not one cannon in place. Indeed it was further suggested that York might easily be taken by a force of only 800 trained soldiers supported by cannon. Attempts were made to address the weaknesses but these only amounted to the expenditure of £1 14s 9d for workmen's wages, and then a further £13 10s 6d, pitifully small amounts.

As the rebels returned to Scotland before being brutally vanquished at the Battle of Culloden, things began to return to normal in York. This close call was to be York's last experience of major land-based conflict. The Duke of Cumberland, the second son of George II and commander of the British army, had been welcomed to York as he headed north to Scotland to take over following another English defeat, this time at Falkirk. Archbishop Herring met the Duke and lent him his own coach to travel as far as Boroughbridge, and the Duke's birthday on April 15th was enthusiastically celebrated in York itself. After the victory at Culloden, the Archbishop wrote to Cumberland to say, 'Give me leave to interrupt you for a moment to congratulate you on this great event in Scotland.' The Corporation also invited the Duke to accept the freedom of the city, to be presented at a lavish feast held in the Precentor's House. Frozen sugar sweetmeats cost £5 13s 6d, champagne £10 16s, and wine £15 6s. Entertainment, presumably music, was an additional £9 9s.

As rebel prisoners were due to arrive at the city, a mob eagerly awaited their coming. They lined the streets for two days in frenzied anticipation with Jacobites arriving from 3rd December onward so that by 7th February 1746 there were 227 prisoners in the city. During the following months, rebel prisoners were moved between various gaols for trial and in October of that year, seventy were found guilty of high treason. Twenty-two Jacobite rebels were executed at York, greeted by loud huzzas from the crowd. Then,

The Duke of York, Prince Frederick Augustus, belonged to the House of Hanover. He was born on 16 August 1763, the son of King George III.

Above left: General Sir Charles Howard KCB, Colonel of the Green Howards, 1738 to 1748.

Above right: Royal Dragoon Guards crest and badge.

in 1747, of the remaining rebels, sixty-six prisoners were sentenced to be transported, and thirty-seven were pardoned but on condition that they enlist in the British army. Some were discharged or else pardoned and at least one prisoner escaped. The final two pardons were issued in 1752, several years after the conflict. This relative leniency at York differed radically from some of the post-rebellion trials such as Somerset's 'bloody assizes' of 1685.

Two heads from executed rebels were placed on Micklegate Bar in 1745, and remained there until 1754 when a York tailor, William Arundel, stole them on 19th February. It was noted that the heads had been taken by 'wicked and disaffected persons, in contempt of the king's authority'. The Corporation's officials were to make 'the strictest enquiry' for those responsible and offered a £10 reward for information. First of all Thomas Wake was arrested and placed in York Castle dungeons, but then John Moffit claimed that Arundel, a man of Irish descent, was responsible. Though bailed with a bond of £300, he was found guilty and gaoled for two years for the theft.

So, by the late 1700s, the role of York in direct ground conflict had been dramatically reduced.

8. THE SECOND WORLD WAR & THE COLD WAR

With its uniquely long timeline of military history and a centre for troops and operations, forces based in York have been involved in conflicts across Britain, Europe and the world since the Romans. In a volume such as this, there is simply no space to consider these engagements in detail beyond the references already presented and brief coverage under military honours. York-based battalions were involved in training and in conflicts for major conflicts in the Crimea, in South Africa, and of course, in the First World War.

However, certain key examples of conflicts are especially significant. In this case, the role of York and its immediate environs in the Second World War stands out as particularly interesting as does its involvement in the Cold War.

The Second World War, 1939–45

Along with being a base for military training and for troops in the area, York was particularly significant as a centre for airbases located in the flatlands around the city and the Vale of York. However, before we venture into the British airbases, one famous or infamous episode for York in the Second World War, was as a target for Luftwaffe reprisals for Allied bombing of historic German towns, the so-called Baedeker Blitz.

The Baedeker Blitz

Being an important location for industry and commerce can come at a high price during times of conflict, something experienced by York over many centuries. However, the damage during the Second World War was especially distressing when, on 29th April 1942, York suffered retaliatory bombing as part of so-called Baedeker Blitz by the German Luftwaffe. Ninety-two people were killed and hundreds injured, with some famous and historic buildings damaged and gutted. The Baedeker Raids occurred from April to June 1942 as retaliation for the Bomber Command attack on the historic German city of Lübeck when more than a thousand people died and the ancient 'Old Town' of timber buildings was virtually destroyed by incendiaries. Hitler's retaliatory raids were named after the *Baedeker* travel guidebooks with old, historic, English cities identified as targets because they were three-starred in the guides.

Military Airfields Around York

The first military airfields around York would have been operational during the First World War and on some of the extensive flatlands of the Vale of York. There is relatively little known about such early sites but far more about those which followed in the Second World War. The area around York at this time has been described as virtually a huge aircraft carrier. The skies over York must have echoed with the noise of heavy bombers gaining altitude prior to heading east and over the North Sea to Germany. At sometimes very short notice, large parcels of countryside were requisitioned by the Air Ministry to construct the necessary airfields and sometimes dummy airfields. Around the airstrips were living quarters and all the necessary infrastructure for flying crews and ground crews from across the country and around the world. Today many of these often short-term airfields are forgotten and some returned to their original farmland uses. Some airfields are still active, some returned to nature, and others ended up in industrial usage, including the wartime buildings.

Acaster Malbis Airfield

This was a bad choice for a flying site because of proximity to the River Ouse and low-lying flatlands prone to mists and fogs that often made operations impossible or at least very dangerous. The site was established in 1942 as part of No. 12 Group, Fighter Command, and a satellite to RAF Church Fenton. The first planes to arrive were Airacobras with No. 601 Unit. This aircraft, one of the principal American fighter planes in service when the United States entered the war, was not popular and technical issues plus a tendency for poor performance in poor weather resulted in serious accidents.

No. 601 gave way to No. 21 Group, Flying Training Command, and No. 15 Advanced Flying Unit with Airspeed Oxfords. However, the poor visibility continued to take its toll

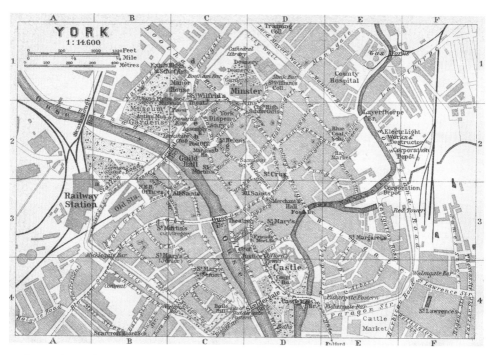

York city plan in the *Baedeker Guide* around 1910 and the trigger for Hitler's retaliatory raids by the Luftwaffe.

on both combat flights and training purposes for which the airfield was soon deemed unsuitable. In 1943, the airfield closed to re-open as a heavy bomber station for part of No. 4 Group, Bomber Command. This latest stage involved construction of concrete runways,

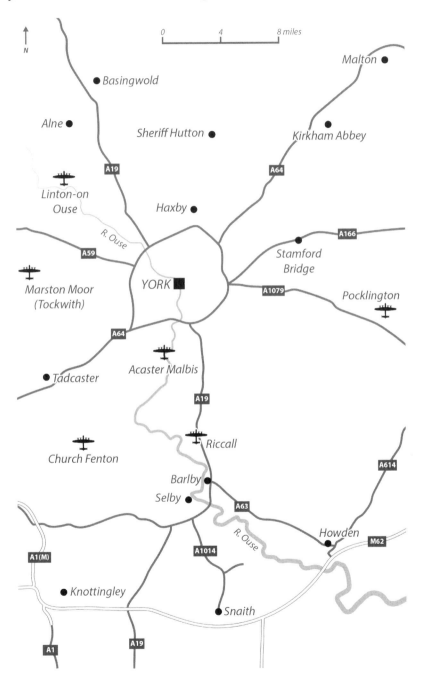

Based in Yorkshire, No. 303 (Polish) Squadron RAF, October 1940. (Photo S. A. Devon / RAF)

hangars and new accommodation blocks. With its recurring problems, the airfield was only used for circuit training by flying crews. Active flights were eventually abandoned and the site became a bomb storage depot. It finally closed down in 1946 and perhaps represents a testament to tenacity in the face of continuing failure.

According to the on-line enthusiasts' guides the site is worth visiting to see features such as the still-remaining control tower and surviving parts of the domestic quarters. The runways survived well after active service but have now been broken up and the land returned to farming.

Marston Moor Airfield (RAF Tockwith)

Close to the famous battlefield, as part of No. 4 Group, Bomber Command, this base opened in 1941 as a heavy bomber conversion training station. The conversion units were equipped with Halifax Mk Is but there seem to have been quite a number of crashes including a Stirling bomber crashing into Tockwith village north-east of the site. All the crew died along with the village postmaster, and fragments from the crash still turn up occasionally in local gardens. The base was decommissioned in 1945 and the site today houses an industrial estate. Much of the original base still exists and is described as one of the best preserved examples of a World War Two airfield in Yorkshire.

Linton-on-Ouse

This was a site picked for development during the airfield's expansion period of the 1930s and many buildings are clearly constructed for longer-term use as opposed to those fabricated in the heat of the war effort. Linton was formally commissioned in 1937 and housed No. 4 Group Headquarters. In 1940, the HQ team transferred to Heslington Hall in York

Hawker Hurricane. (Photo Airwolfhound)

Avro Lancaster bomber. (Photo Ronnie Macdonald)

itself, leaving Linton with operational functions. Later that year, the first arrivals took place of four-engine bombers with 35 Squadron Halifaxes from Leeming. These airfield sites were obvious targets for German counter-bombing, and despite the extensive use of decoys and camouflage, remained vulnerable. So in May 1941, Linton was hit by a German bombing raid, receiving significant damage and casualties including the station commander.

During 1942, Linton was passed to the Canadian Group, in 1943, transferring to No. 6 Group RCAF. At this point it became No. 62 (Beaver) Base Station and acquired sub-stations at East Moor and Tholthorpe. The first group to arrive was No. 426 (Thunderbird) Squadron which started conversion to the Lancaster Mk II with Hercules engines. In August 1943, 426 was joined by No. 408 (Goose) Squadron from Leeming.

At the end of the war in Europe, No. 408 Squadron transferred to the Tiger Force in the Far East for use against Japan. They moved back to Canada with their Lancaster Mk Xs but never reached Japan itself because the war ended. They disbanded at Greenwood, Nova Scotia, in September 1945, a long way from York!

No. 426 Squadron remained closer to home, in May 1945 being transferred to No. 47 Squadron, Group Transport Command, and moving to Driffield in East Yorkshire. Linton returned to the RAF and for a short while was part of No. 4 Group, Transport Command but in 1946 passed on to Fighter Command. It was then home to a number of fighter aircraft and squadrons until in 1957 it was clear that the site could not be converted to take newer, high-performance, jet fighters then coming into service.

Armourers 'bombing up' a Handley Page Halifax Mk II of No. 405 Squadron RCAF at Pocklington in Yorkshire, August 1942. (photo Forward (F/O / RAF via IWM))

A Halifax crew pose on their aircraft that was hit by a 'friendly bomb' during a raid over Cologne in June 1943. (Photo RAF via IWM)

Linton was briefly mothballed prior to re-opening as part of Flying Training Command with No. 1 Flying Training School moving there from Syerston. Until 1969, the base trained students from both the RAF and the Fleet Air Arm but the latter was transferred to Church Fenton. Still an operational airfield, Linton is the training base for future RAF pilots. As a working site, many original airbase buildings from World War Two still exist.

Riccall

Riccall Airfield, RAF Riccall, or Skipwith Common Airfield, was built in 1942 with three concrete and asphalt runways, six T2 and one B1 hangars. It opened in December the same year as a secondary site associated with RAF Marston Moor. On opening it already had Halifax conversion units of No. 76 Squadron and No. 78 Squadron that arrived in September. By October 1942, they merged to become the 1658 Heavy Conversion Unit (HCU) with 158 Conversion Unit also arriving in November to form 'C' Flight 1658 with a total of thirty-two Halifax bombers based at the airfield. Riccall was the training ground for many thousands of aircrew flying Halifax squadrons but there was a heavy price with seventy-two planes lost during the period. The 1658 Heavy Conversion Unit disbanded close to the end of the war in Europe with Riccall becoming home to 1332 Transport Conversion Unit. The base then flew Avro Yorks and Short Stirlings converted to transportation roles.

When this use ended on 7th November 1945, Riccall was mothballed as a site for storage with just maintenance units until final closure in February 1957. The land then passed back into agriculture or developed as birch-wood and heath. Some buildings still remain though much was demolished after closure. The site is probably one of the easiest wartime airfields to visit since much of the area is open access. A lot of the old runway is still visible along with the perimeter track and some buildings including accommodation units. Interestingly, the former bomb dump remains within Skipwith Common Nature Reserve.

Pocklington

The Pocklington airbase was actually developed during the 1930s' expansion plans for military airfields, but it was not until 1941 that it opened for No. 4 Group, Bomber Command. Sometime after opening, No. 405 Squadron RCAF with Wellington bombers also moved in from Driffield to convert crews to Halifax bombers. Indeed, the Halifax B Mk IIs became operational soon afterwards and this was the first Canadian unit to fly them in action. In April 1942, No. 405 Squadron switched with No. 102 Squadron who moved to Pocklington from Topcliffe and during 1944, the latter changed from Halifax B Mk II bombers to Mark IIIs in preparation for the Normandy D-Day landings. Finally, in 1945, No. 102 moved to transport duties using Liberators and left Pocklington in September, the base closing in 1946. Much of the site is now farmland but the hangars remain as part of an industrial estate. One original runway is still used by Pocklington Gliding Club.

Church Fenton

The airbase at Church Fenton was designated a fighter station as part of the pre-war expansion scheme and formed part of No. 12 Group, Fighter Command. In 1937, the site opened with a grass airstrip and No. 72 Squadron equipped with Gloster Gladiators and No. 213 Squadron with Gloster Gauntlets. On the outbreak of war, the site passed to No. 13 Group, Fighter Command and No. 72 Squadron converted to the Spitfire Mk I. The latter soon decanted out to Leconfield to be replaced at Church Fenton by a detachment from No. 245 Squadron coming the other way from Leconfield and the re-formed No. 242 Squadron manning Hurricanes. The primary role of this base during the initial stages of the war was the protection of the East Coast and the nearby towns. During the Battle of Britain, squadrons were despatched to Church Fenton for relief and re-equipping. One particular claim to fame and glory was the award of the Victoria Cross to Flight Lieutenant J. B. Nicholson, the only such award to Fighter Command during the war. The airfield was a fighter station until in 1959 it passed to Flying Training Command. In 1962, No. 7 Flying Training School was established with Jet Provost planes and today is the base for Grob Tutor aircraft of the University Air Squadron. It is now Leeds East Airport Church Fenton.

The Cold War

In the aftermath of World War Two, the major powers slipped seamlessly into the so-called 'Cold War', essentially a political and military stand-off between Western and Soviet ideologies. During the 1950s and 1960s, the HQ of No. 20 Group, Royal Observer Corps transferred to newly constructed facilities in the 'York Cold War Bunker' built in 1961 in the Holgate part of the city. The York Cold War Bunker was two storey and semi-underground; its function in the possible event of nuclear war was monitoring nuclear explosions and any associated fallout in Yorkshire. This was one of around thirty such installations in the United Kingdom. Between 1961 and 1991 the building operated as the regional HQ and control centre for No. 20 Group York of the Royal Observer Corps. The site opened on 16th December 1961 and remained operational up to 1991. On closure, it became a Scheduled Monument owned and managed by English Heritage, opening in 2006 as a museum.

During the Cold War, the base was able to support up to sixty local volunteer members of the Royal Observer Corps, with a ten-man scientific warning team from the United Kingdom Warning and Monitoring Organization. Their role would be to collate details of nuclear bombs exploded across the UK, tracking radioactive fallout, and warning the public of associated dangers. The York centre is now the only operational-condition ROC control building remaining; others were demolished, sold, or are derelict. The fully restored York Cold War Bunker includes air filtration and generating plant, a kitchen and canteen, plus dormitories, radio and landline communication equipment, 1980s' specialist, advanced computers, and the operations room boasting vertical, illuminated, Perspex maps.

A typical RAF control room in an underground bunker. This one is at Holmpton, East Riding. (Photo Michael King)

9. SERVICE, HONOURS & AWARDS

One remarkable military honour for York was when, in 1971, it became an army 'Saluting Station'. As such, the army based here fires a gun five times a year to salute significant commemorations such as the Queen's Birthday. The date marking this recognition was 1,900 years of a major military presence in York. This is a long history of military service and importance back to at least the Romans. It is actually very hard to fairly attribute York's military service and battle honours over the centuries, in part because the time-line of action is so long and in part because of mergers and changes between regiments and units over recent centuries. Furthermore, while York has not been the official base for all the region's 'Yorkshire' regiments, it has been a centre for many of them at various times and in a variety of conflicts. The list below therefore includes those honours both directly and less directly associated with the city:

- Nine Years' War: Namur 1695
- War of the Spanish Succession: Blenheim, Ramillies, Oudenaarde, Malplaquet
- War of the Austrian Succession: Louisburg, Dettingen
- Seven Years' War: Quebec 1759, Martinique 1762, Havana
- American War of Independence: St Lucia 1778, Martinique 1794 and 1809
- War of the First Coalition: Tournay, Belle Isle
- Second Anglo-Maratha War: Hindoostan, Mysore, Ally Ghur, Delhi 1803, Leswaree, Deig
- Fourth Anglo-Mysore War: Seringapatam
- Napoleonic Wars: Corunna, Nive, Peninsula, Guadaloupe 1810, Waterloo
- Jat War 1825–26: Siege of Bhurtpore 1825-26 (Bharatpur)
- Crimean War: Alma, Inkerman, Sevastopol, Abyssinia
- New Zealand War: New Zealand
- Second Anglo-Afghan War: Tirah, Afghanistan 1879–80
- Second Boer War: Relief of Ladysmith, Relief of Kimberley, Paardeberg, South Africa 1900–02
- First World War: Mons, Le Cateau, Retreat from Mons, Battle of the Marne 1914 and 1918, Aisne 1914 and 1918, Armentières 1914, La Bassée 1914, Ypres 1914, 1915, 1917 and 1918, Langemarck 1914 and 1917, Gheluvelt, Nonne Bosschen, Neuve Chapelle, Hill 60, Gravenstafel, St. Julien, Frezenberg, Bellewaarde, Aubers, Festubert, Hooge 1915, Loos, Somme 1916 and 1918, Albert 1916 and 1918, Bazentin, Delville Wood, Pozières, Flers-Courcelette, Morval, Thiepval, Le Transloy, Ancre Heights, Ancre 1916, Arras 1916, 1917 and 1918, Scarpe 1917 and 1918, Arleux, Oppy, Bullecourt, Hill 70, Messines 1917 and 1918, Pilckem, Menin Road, Polygon Wood, Broodseinde, Poelcappelle, Passchendaele, Cambrai 1917 and 1918, St Quentin, Bapaume 1918, Rosieres, Ancre 1918, Villiers Bretonneux, Lys, Estaires, Hazebrouck, Bailleul, Kemmel, Bethune, Scherpenberg,

Marne 1918, Tardenois, Amiens, Drocourt-Quéant, Hindenburg Line, Havrincourt, Epéhy, Canal du Nord, St Quentin Canal, Beaurevoir, Selle, Valenciennes, Sambre, France and Flanders 1914–18, Piave, Vittorio Veneto, Italy 1917–18, Struma, Doiran 1917, Macedonia 1915–18, Suvla, Landing at Suvla, Scimitar Hill, Gallipoli 1915, Egypt 1915–1916, Archangel 1918,

- Third Anglo-Afghan War: Afghanistan 1919
- Second World War: Otta, Norway 1940, Withdrawal to Escaut, Defence of Arras, French Frontier 1940, Ypres-Comines Canal, Dunkirk 1940, St Valery-en-Caux, Normandy Landing, Tilly sur Seulles, Odon, Fontenay Le Pesnil, Caen, Bourguebus Ridge, Troarn, Mont Pincon, St Pierre La Vielle, Gheel, Nederrijn, Aam, Venraij, Rhineland, Schaddenhof, Brinkum, Bremen, North-West Europe 1940 and 1944-45, Jebel Defeis, Keren, Ad Teclescan, Abyssinia 1940–41, Gazala, Cauldron, Mersa Matruh, Defence of Alamein Line, El Alamein, Mareth, Wadi ZigZaou, Akarit, North Africa 1940–42, 1942–43 and 1943, Banana Ridge, Medjez Plain, Gueriat el Atach Ridge, Tunis, Djebel Bou Aoukaz 1943, North Africa 1943, Primasole Bridge, Landing in Sicily, Lentini, Sicily 1943, Minturno, Anzio, Campoleone, Rome, Monte Ceco, Italy 1943–44 and 43–45, Sittang 1942, Pegu 1942, Paungde, Yenangyaung 1942, North Arakan, Maungdaw, Defence of Sinzweya, Imphal, Bishenpur, Kanglantonbi, Kohima, Meiktila, Capture of Meiktila, Defence of Meiktila, Rangoon Road, Pyawbwe, Arakan beaches, Chindits 1944, Burma Campaign (1942–44).
- Korean War: The Hook 1953, Korean War 1952–53 (Theatre Honour)
- Iraq War: Iraq 2003 (Theatre Honour)

The arrangement for attribution and display of battle honours is complex, especially when mergers and reorganizations happen. In this context, infantry regiments can display forty-three battle honours from the two World Wars on the Queen's Colour and forty-six from other conflicts on the Regimental Colour. With amalgamations the Yorkshire Regiment selected these from the accumulated honours of its three constituent regiments. Those chosen were:

On the Queen's Colour
Mons; Marne 1914, 1918; Aisne 1914, 1918; Armentières 1914; Ypres 1914, 1915, 1917, 1918; Hill 60 1915; Loos; Somme 1916, 1918; Arras 1917, 1918; Cambrai 1917, 1918; Lys; Tardenois; Selle; Valenciennes; Piave; Vittoria Veneto; Doiran 1917; Suvla; Gallipoli 1915; Norway 1940; Dunkirk; St Valery en Caux; Normandy Landing; Odon; Fontenay le Pesnil; Schaddenhof; North-West Europe 1940, 1944–45; Keren; Gazala; El Alamein; Mareth; Akarit; Djebel Bou Aoukaz 1943; Sicily 1943; Minturno; Anzio; Monte Ceco; Sittang 1942, 1945; Pegu 1942; Defence of Sinweya; Imphal; Meiktila; Burma 1942–45

On the Regimental Colour
Namur 1695; Blenheim; Ramillies; Oudenarde; Malplaquet; Dettingen; Louisburg; Quebec 1759; Bellisle; Martinique 1762; Havannah; St Lucia 1778; Martinique 1794, 1809;

Tournay; Mysore; Seringapatam; Ally Ghur; Delhi 1803; Leswarree; Dieg; Corunna; Guadaloupe 1810; Java; Nive; Peninsula; Waterloo; Bhurtpore; Alma; Inkerman; Sevastopol; New Zealand; Abyssinia; Afghanistan 1879–80; Tirah; Relief of Kimberley; Paardeburg; Relief of Ladysmith; South Africa 1899–1902; Afghanistan 1919; Korea 1952–53; The Hook 1953; Iraq 2003

The regimental colours also have four emblems from earlier regiments:

- The White Horse of Hanover – displayed top right; from the Prince of Wales's Own Regiment of Yorkshire
- The Star of Brunswick – displayed bottom left; from Prince of Wales's Own Regiment of Yorkshire
- The Dannebrog Cross – displayed bottom right, from the Green Howards
- The Elephant & Howdah – displayed bottom centre, from the Duke of Wellington's Regiment

Soldiers' memorial and York Minster.

The Battalion's Roman numeral is in the top left corner of each flag, and the Cross of St George as the background is unique to the Yorkshire Regiment.

One individual honour that has been briefly mentioned was the award of the Victoria Cross to York-trained Flight Lieutenant J. B. (Eric James Brindley) Nicolson, the only such award to RAF Fighter Command during the Second World War. Nicolson was 23 years old when his squadron, No. 249, moved south from its Yorkshire base. On 16th August 1940, flying from Boscombe Down near Southampton, Nicolson's Hawker Hurricane was fired on by a Messerschmitt Bf 110. Injured in one eye and a foot, and with his engine damaged and alight, as he struggled to bail out, he spotted another Messerschmitt. Nicolson squeezed back into the pilot's seat and fired on the enemy plane until it went down. He then left his own plane and parachuted to relative safety in a field – although he was shot at by the Home Guard who assumed he was German. By 1944, Nicolson was a squadron leader and Commanding Officer No. 27 Squadron, flying Bristol Beaufighters over Burma and was further awarded the Distinguished Flying Cross. Sadly, he died in action on 2nd May 1945, when as a wing commander and an observer in an RAF B-24 Liberator of No. 355 Squadron, his plane caught fire and crashed into the Bay of Bengal; his body never found.

The Green Howards' Memorial, York.

Above: Commemorated in a steam train, the Green Howard steam engine at York Station in the 1950s.

Left: First World War soldier 'Cyril' from the Princess Alexandra Yorkshire Regiment.

Associated with York by birth or by military base, are seven Great War heroes who received the Victoria Cross. Their exploits are described by Robert Hamilton in his book, *Victoria Cross Heroes of World War One.*

Charles Hull, a Harrogate postman, on 5th September 1915 rescued Captain Learoyd from certain death at the hands of tribesmen at Hafiz Kor on the North West Frontier. The officer's horse had been shot and Hull caught him up onto his own horse and carried him to safety.

In September 1916, Captain Archie White, from Boroughbridge, was commanding troops holding the southern and western faces at Stuff Redoubt in France against heavy German assaults. Though low on supplies and ammunition, White personally led a counter-attack to clear out the enemy.

Under heavy fire, Lieutenant Donald Bell of Harrogate rushed across open land and attacked a machine gun, shooting the operator with his revolver and destroying the gun and other personnel with grenades, an act that saved many lives and ensured the success of the attack. Bell said he believed God had been watching over him but, within five days, he was killed during an attack on another machine gun at Contalmaison.

Near the small village of Roeux, Private Tom Dresser of the Green Howards, on 12th May 1917, despite severe injuries and exhaustion, succeeded in carrying an important message from HQ to the front line. His act proved vital to his battalion.

On 10th April 1918, stretcher-bearer Arthur Poulter, from East Witton near Leyburn, at Erquinghem-Lys in France, carried wounded soldiers on his back under heavy artillery and machine-gun fire. Shortly afterwards during another engagement he bandaged forty men whilst under fire and was himself seriously injured by a bullet that hit him in the head near the eye socket. Invalided home, he regained his sight and worked as a tailor. He died in Leeds at the age of sixty-two.

Corporal Harry Blanshard Wood, of Newton-on-Derwent, took command of his platoon after his sergeant was killed at St Python, France, on 13th October 1918. He was vital in the action to cross the River Selle and take control of the village and, under heavy fire, repelled several enemy counter-attacks.

Lieutenant Colonel Bertram Best-Dunkley was from York. On 31st July 1917, the first day of the Battle of Passchendaele, his battalion came under small-arms attack from German positions that had been assumed to be Allied forces. Best-Dunkley personally led his men against the enemy and was successful in neutralizing them and, despite being wounded, holding the position against German counter-attack. He died of his wounds just a few days later, aged twenty-seven. He is buried at Mendinghem Military Cemetery near Ypres, Belgium.

10. THE MILITARY HERITAGE

York has been the home of soldiers from many nations and forces over the centuries. However, in recent times the city and the area around has been the headquarters of a number of specific regiments. The main barracks and their histories are briefly described below though the major facilities will mostly close within the next decade or so.

Left: Armoured car on show at the military tattoo in 1929.

Below: The new Soldiers' Institute at York, 1887.

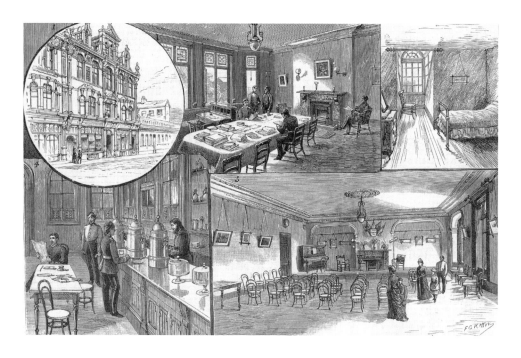

Imphal (Fulford) Barracks

The cavalry barracks was built in Fulford in response to the threat of the French Revolution and war with Napoleon. Completed in 1795, the early buildings are now mostly demolished, and infantry barracks were built between 1877 and 1878 as part of the Cardwell Reforms to increase localization of British military forces. The latter were home to the 14th Regiment of Foot which, following the Childers Reforms, transferred from Bradford Moor Barracks to Fulford and became the West Yorkshire Regiment in 1881. With the Cardwell Reforms, two battalions of the 25th (Sussex) Regiment of Foot had a base at the barracks but the Childers Reforms changed that regiment into the King's Own Scottish Borderers at Berwick Barracks. The base was renamed in the 1950s as the Imphal Barracks in honour of the West Yorkshire Regiment's role at the Second World War Battle of Imphal, Manipur, India, in spring of 1944. In 1958, the barracks also became the base for Northern Command and the home of the Prince of Wales's Own Regiment of Yorkshire as the West Yorkshire Regiment amalgamated with the East Yorkshire Regiment. Northern Command was then disbanded in 1972 to be replaced by North East District and in 1982 the barracks were also the base for the 2nd Division. Then in turn, in 1991, the North East District was disbanded and the 2nd Division now merged with Scotland District,

B7 Squad PTC, Fulford Barracks, April 1943.

York infantry barracks, June 1914.

moved its headquarters to Craigiehall, near Edinburgh in April 2001. In June 2006, the formation of the Yorkshire Regiment was celebrated and the new divisional headquarters of 6th Division marked its formation with a parade and flag presentation at Imphal Barracks on 5th August 2008. There was a focus on preparations for Afghanistan during summer 2009, and the divisional headquarters was significantly reinforced and transformed into Combined Joint Task Force 6 before deploying to Afghanistan as Regional Command South in November 2009. This divisional HQ closed in April 2011, the barracks becoming the base for 15th Infantry Brigade until 1st December 2014. They then joined the former 4th Mechanized Brigade, forming the 4th Infantry Brigade and HQ North East in Catterick. From 1st June 2015, Imphal was the base for the 1st (United Kingdom) Division. Finally, in November 2016, the Ministry of Defence announced the closure of the site in 2031, ending a centuries-long presence.

The barracks was formerly served by a horse-drawn, narrow-gauge railway running from the Ordnance Wharf on the River Ouse parallel to Hospital Fields Road. Munitions and other supplies delivered by the schooner *Princess*, also called the 'Powder boat', could be taken directly to the army depot.

Strensall Camp

Strensall is based a few miles north-east of York close to Strensall Common which is now a Special Area of Conservation with a large area of important lowland heathland habitat. Heaths and moors have long been favoured for military use and the army still has firing

On the march at Strensall Common.

Soldiers at Strensall Common Camp.

Strensall Camp, 1926.

Strensall Common Camp.

The Durham Regiment at Strensall Common.

ranges and training areas belonging to the Ministry of Defence. In 1884, the camp was established by the War Office for training combat troops on around 1,800 acres of land. The associated barracks were renamed the Queen Elizabeth II Barracks in the 1950s and as the Yorkshire Brigade Depot, became the main regional centre for infantry training in the 1960s. In 1968, the site was the depot of the King's Division, and it was here on 11th June 1974 that the Provisional Irish Republican Army successfully planted and detonated bombs, fortunately without loss of life.

It is now the base for the King's Division Recruiting Team, HQ 2 Medical Brigade, Army Medical Services (Force Troops Command), 34 Field Hospital, the Garrison Dental Centre, HQ Strensall Training Centre, 4 Cadet Training Team, the Army Youth Team, HQ Yorkshire (North and West) the Army Cadet Force, the Military Police Guarding Service Defence Platoon, and various associated smaller units. However, in November 2016, the Ministry of Defence announced the site's closure in 2021 terminating nearly 150 years of military usage.

Duncombe Barracks, Burton Stone Lane

This has been the base site for army reservists and the military intelligence unit, Military Intelligence Battalion, plus the department of motor vehicles, but was notified of closure in 2013 with the reservists moving to the Fulford Road, Worsley Barracks, with the 4th Battalion the Yorkshire Regiment and Y Squadron the Queen's Own Yeomanry.

Worsley Barracks

The modern TA barracks is a purpose-built facility close to York centre with meeting hall and rooms and modern training facilities. The site has multiple usages and includes a firing range suitable for small weapons.

York's Operational Forces: The Yorkshire Regiment (14th/15th, 19th & 33rd/76th Foot) (Abbreviated YORKS)

The city has long-standing associations with many and varied military groups over the years. The Yorkshire Regiment was created in 2006 from the merging of three famous northern regiments with over 300 years of military history. The heritage of earlier regiments carries into the modern force with two regular and one reserve battalion. However, the close association with York is much reduced. 1st Battalion, equipped with Warrior armoured fighting vehicles, is based at Warminster, and 2nd Battalion, with Foxhound protected patrol vehicles, is at Catterick. The 4th Battalion, the Army Reserve unit, is based at various sites in Yorkshire and Teesside, training in light infantry roles and able to mobilize along with the Regular Army.

The current regiment is made up from three Yorkshire Infantry Regiments: The Prince of Wales's Own Regiment of Yorkshire (14th/15th Foot), The Green Howards (Alexandra, Princess of Wales's Own Yorkshire Regiment) (19th Foot) and The Duke of Wellington's Regiment (West Riding) (33rd/76th Foot) and associated Army Reserve units.

York Military Sunday celebrations and parade, 30 April 1905.

Right: Military Sunday, 1920s, with Hilda Macrae.

Below: York Military Tattoo, 1929.

Testing new technology: a hovercraft designed to beat the swamps is tested at Imphal Barracks, March 1961.

The history of the Yorkshire Regiments goes back as far as 1685 with James Stuart, Duke of York, becoming King James II and needing an army to deal with the south-western rebellion of the Duke of Monmouth. Also known as the 'Revolt of the West' or the 'West Country rebellion', this was an attempt by the protestant James Scott, 1st Duke of Monmouth, an illegitimate son of the recently deceased King Charles II, to claim the throne by usurping the Catholic King James II. The rebellion ended on 6th July 1685 with the catastrophic defeat of Monmouth's army at the Battle of Sedgemoor. Monmouth was executed for treason on 15th July 1685 and many rebels were executed or transported following the 'Bloody Assizes' overseen by Judge Jeffreys, who, apparently suffering from severe piles, was both quick and brutal in his judgements. James was able to hold on to power but only until 1688, and the coup by the protestant William of Orange, the so-called 'Glorious Revolution'.

The Yorkshire regiment remains closely associated with York and Yorkshire with a motto 'One County, One Regiment, Our Family'. In the new infantry structure, this is presently the only line unit (infantry or rifles) drawn from a single geographical county. However, in the *Army 2020* defence review the regiment did lose a battalion.

4th Battalion (Abbreviated to 4 YORKS)

This is the reserve infantry battalion in Yorkshire and Teesside and part of 4th Infantry Brigade and HQ North East. The function of the battalion is support to the Regular Army and especially the Yorkshire Regiment. It is based out of the Worsley Barracks in Fulford but also operates from Army Reserve centres over the countywide regimental footprint. There are companies in Scarborough, Sheffield, Barnsley, Hull, Leeds, Beverley, Huddersfield, Middlesbrough, and York.

The current regimental recruiting area includes virtually all the historic county of Yorkshire with the three ridings, East, North and West. Excluded are parts of eastern South Yorkshire and the south-east of West Yorkshire. Nevertheless, recruitment does in practice extend beyond the formal area and would-be soldiers especially from north-east England and the Commonwealth are welcomed.

The current phases of reorganization, mergers and closures mean a continuing reduction of York's defence role. Combat-related functions will all but end by 2030. The closures are not without controversy with York Central Labour MP Rachael Maskell at the time stating in the York press that the Imphal Barracks closure would have a massive impact on the city and the economy. In civilian jobs alone, 365 will be lost. However, situated in or close to York, Imphal and Strensall are large sites, with major potential as prime real estate for re-development as residential, office or retail usage.

The Prince of Wales's Own Regiment of Yorkshire Museum

This regimental museum of the Royal Dragoon Guards and the Yorkshire Regiment, in York city centre close to the Jorvik Viking Centre and near Clifford's Tower, is now called the York Army Museum. The displays include artefacts and photographs relating to regimental histories from the Crimean War, the North-West Frontier of India, the Boer War, to the Great War and the Second World War. There are medals and decorations, uniforms, weapons, memorabilia, and of course, a regimental gift shop. The Yorkshire Museum and York Castle Museum also have extensive collections and exhibitions relating to military history and the Yorkshire regiments through history, and 'Jorvik' itself tells the early stories.

11. THE WALLS & OTHER DEFENCES

This account closes with a more detailed look at what the tourist sees today. For the modern visitor to York, the city walls are one of its most striking features, even though they are only a fragment of their former glory. They are now a Scheduled Ancient Monument and Grade I Listed Building, though over the centuries they have had a chequered history. By comparison with most medieval towns and cities, York's defences remain relatively intact. As detailed in the wonderful and comprehensive volume on the *City of York, Volume II, The Defences* (1972), York is remarkable not only for the features which remain, but also

Plan of the city from the 1970s' *York* guidebook.

for the plans and images of the walls as they once were and the sections that have been lost. It is unusual for a town or city to possess such a remarkable record.

While the walls we see today date back to Roman times, originally built of earth and wood in 71 AD, they have had phases of destruction, rebuilding and enhancement. For example, in the third and fourth centuries AD they were rebuilt in stone as the significance of York as a Roman-British centre grew. Following abandonment by the legions, the Anglo-Saxons patched up the former Roman defences, and the later Vikings and Normans replaced much of the defensive structure with massive earth ramparts. Finally the York city walls were rebuilt in stone in the thirteenth century to defend the city from marauding Scots.

The later history of the walls includes when they were partly repaired in preparation for siege in 1745 when Bonnie Prince Charlie led the Jacobite Rebellion. Fortunately, since by this time they were considered unfit for defensive purposes, they were not put to the test as the Jacobites took a different route. Indeed, the final defensive use of the walls was in 1757, when protestors angered by taxes to support the militia rioted and threatened the city. By the late 1700s, the walls were falling apart and becoming tumble-down, and in 1800 the city resolved to sponsor the passing of an Act of Parliament to allow the demolition of the walls but the government and even King George III himself, apparently refused to give assent to the bill. Faced by this refusal, York Council decided to attain their objective by increments. Indeed, many local councils went about demolishing walls and medieval gateways in order to free up the town from the straightjackets of the earlier layout. Gateways in particular caused increasing difficulties for urban traffic as numbers of people, animals, and vehicles increased. One casualty was in 1807 when Skeldergate Postern was demolished. However, this caused ructions as Archbishop Markham sued the council because of lost income from tolls he was entitled to charge during Lammastide, a harvest festival to celebrate the annual wheat harvest, usually on 1st August. Following this costly episode, future demolitions were approached rather more cautiously. Although the Council was steadfast in its desire to remove the walls and the gates, there was growing opposition. York-born artist William Etty RA was among those leading the campaign to halt further removals and to restore the walls and gates as an amenity. In 1826, one of the most eminent and popular writers of the time, Sir Walter Scott, even offered to walk from Edinburgh to London if that would serve to safeguard Micklegate Bar Barbican. The campaign was successful in saving much of the walls, the gates and at least parts of the Castle. These are mostly now in the ownership of York City Council, and those that remain are listed as Ancient Monuments. Much was lost but it could have been far worse as was the case for many towns and cities. Today, with guidance and support from English Heritage these structures are maintained by York City Council though conservation work often requires specialist masons and others brought in as contractors.

While they were in active use, the bars and posterns were continuously manned. Originally with resident 'Bar Keepers', up to the latter part of the eighteenth century, they were closed between dusk and dawn. At this time, many towns operated strict curfews after dark as some degree of security against thieves and vagabonds. Curfew bells would be rung at either 8 o'clock or 9 o'clock in the evening and, among other things, all lights had to be put out. This was largely because of the risk of fire – with buildings of wood and thatch, and lights with naked flames. At York on Sundays, the city gates were also closed twice daily in order to stop townsfolk slipping out to nearby country ale-houses rather than going to church as was expected. Other additions to security included, from 1501, special door knockers at the bars for the use of 'Scots and other vagabonds and rascals' who had to knock before being allowed entry to the city. There is some suggestion, though unsubstantiated, that there was a statute allowing a citizen to shoot a Scotsman on sight, provided he did it with a crossbow. Furthermore, it is also alleged that the said statute has not as yet been repealed.

The Roman walls

The original walls were constructed about 71 AD, as a fort or *castra* on around fifty acres close to the River Ouse. This rectangle of walls was part of the fort's defence and the walls existing today follow the line and foundations, at least in part, of the originals in that same area: the western corner and Multangular Tower now in the Museum Gardens, the north-western and north-eastern sections of wall between Bootham Bar and Monk Bar, and the wall between Monk Bar and the Merchant Taylors' Hall with the lower sections of the Roman wall's eastern corner visible in the remaining wall.

The Multangular Tower is the finest example of upstanding Roman remains in York. The structure is a projecting nine-sided bastion, and was built around 300 AD, perhaps intended to house a ballister-style catapult to fire at enemy ships should they attack up the Ouse. The tower was built as part of a series of eight similar defensive positions around the walls of the original Roman fortress, though the structure today has been much altered by medieval and later constructions. The walls of the fort were most likely built for Septimius Severus, but the Multangular Tower is a later addition, probably by Constantine the Great around 310–320 AD. It has ten sides including access openings to the rear.

The Vikings occupied York in 867 AD and by then the Roman defences were mostly dilapidated. Except for the Multangular Tower all the other towers were destroyed but the defensive walls, mostly of earth and timber, were to some extent repaired enough to survive in part to the medieval.

However, most of the city walls that encompassed the medieval city date from the twelfth to the fourteenth centuries. There was then piecemeal demolition and rebuilding with some late reconstruction carried out in the nineteenth century. From the eastern corner of the Roman walls, the medieval structure continues to Layerthorpe Bridge and then to the King's Fishpool. The latter was a marshy area caused by the Norman damming of the River Foss to give protection so that no walls were needed. The city walls carry on past the River Foss which is now canalized beyond the brick-built Red Tower, southward and westward round the Walmgate and end at one final tower, the Fishergate Postern. This is close by York Castle which of course in earlier times had its own very substantial defensive walls and a moat. There is a short section of wall west

Clifford's Tower and the Castlegate Postern by F. Place, about 1680.

York city walls and the Minster.

of Tower Gardens and this ends with Davy Tower which is again a brick-built tower, this time by the River Ouse. The original line of the wall was up to the Castle walls and a postern on Tower Street.

Past the River Ouse, the walls run to Skeldergate, which also once had a postern tower long since removed, and then up past Baile Hill. Here they turn right and carry on north-west, running alongside what is now the Inner Ring Road. Before the railway station, the walls go right again to continue in a north-easterly direction and terminate with Barker Tower back again on the River Ouse. Barker Tower formerly had a metal chain slung across the river and parallel to Lendal Bridge which is a nineteenth-century construction. A further short run of wall connects to what is today the Museum Gardens entrance, and to the Multangular Tower and line of the original Roman walls.

The Bars & Gates

The walls are punctuated by four main gatehouses, or bars: Bootham, Monk, Walmgate and Micklegate. These controlled traffic in medieval times, and were used to extract tolls, as well as being defensive positions in times of war. In more modern times, city gates became problematic as urban congestion grew and almost all have been removed. York's bars are therefore now of international significance.

Bootham Bar

Though it has some eleventh-century stonework, Bootham Bar was mostly constructed in the fourteenth century and then added to in the nineteenth. The site is also on the location of the Roman *porta principalis dextra* or the north-western gate of Roman Eboracum. The name Bootham Bar is derived from the twelfth-century 'barram de Bootham', which means the bar at the booths i.e. the market booths located nearby. In 1835, the loss of its barbican was one of the causalities of the nineteenth-century demolitions.

Bootham has some claim for notoriety since it was here that severed heads of rebels and traitors were stuck on spikes following the hanging, drawing and quartering of their owners. The custom was for the execution to be undertaken either at York Castle or on Knavesmire and then the four quarters of the bodies were set on four of the main bars of York, and the head on Micklegate. However, on some occasions when Micklegate was already full, then Bootham might be used, or even the Foss or Ouse bridge.

York has many stories associated with such practices, such as that of Harry 'Hotspur' Percy, who died in 1403 fighting at the Battle of Shrewsbury during the rebellion against King Henry IV. Hotspur's body was interred at Whitchurch but it was still said that 'Hotspur lived' and to end such rumours his corpse was exhumed for public display in Shrewsbury Market. Finally, the remains were ground with salt between two millstones to both flatten and preserve, and then they were hanged, drawn and quartered. The quarters were despatched to London, Chester, Newcastle and Bristol, but his head went to ... York.

Bootham Bar by J. Halfpenny, about 1807.

Monk Bar

Of all the bars, Monk Bar, a four-storey gatehouse constructed in the early fourteenth century, is the most elaborate and also the tallest. The structure which replaced the twelfth-century Munecagate, is actually a self-contained miniature fortress, with each

Monk Bar by H. Earp, about 1820.

floor able to be defended independently. The site is near the Roman gate *porta decumana* which is shown by a slight dip in the earthen rampart. Modern Monk Bar has a small museum called the Richard III Experience and importantly this bar still has a working portcullis. Its winding gear is still intact and even up until the First World War, it was lowered on Sunday afternoons. It was finally closed in 1953 to celebrate Queen Elizabeth's coronation, but the old ropes broke, sending the portcullis crashing to earth where it was embedded in road below. The job of repair and raising the portcullis took several days and it has not been lowered since. The machicolations, or 'murder holes', openings in the vault of the gateway, allowed stones, burning objects, or boiling liquids to be dropped onto would-be attackers.

Walmgate Bar

Walmgate Bar, formerly called Walbegate, perhaps after an Anglo-Scandinavian personal name, is mostly fourteenth century though the innermost gateway is twelfth century. Walmgate's most significant feature is its barbican, the only one of the York structures to survive the demolitions, and indeed, the only one left in the whole of England. With fifteenth-century oak doors, an Elizabethan house in the gate was still occupied as recently as 1957. The bar has Roman stone columns supporting it, though they were in part changed around 1584 when the wood-constructed extension was built to enhance the bar keeper's accommodation. It is suggested that the rooftop railings were to keep the pigs in (many urban dwellers kept pigs as an important part of the domestic economy, and the bar keeper, no exception to this, kept his on the roof).

Walmgate Bar in the 1930s.

Walmgate Bar with barbican in the early 1900s.

It has been necessary to repair and restore Walmgate over the centuries as various sieges took their toll, especially the rebellion of 1489 when together with Fishergate Bar, Walmgate was burned by taxation protestors, and then during the Siege of York in the English Civil War in 1644. The structure suffered damage from heavy cannon-fire and the barbican still sags in the left-hand (north) wall due to a mine excavated during the siege. This necessitated extensive repairs in 1648, but, by 1840, it was again suffering from general neglect.

Over the decades, Walmgate has had many uses other than defensive, and was the last York bar to be lived in, up until around 1960. It has since been a bookshop, a Scout room, a rock band practice room, and a coffee shop.

Micklegate Bar

The name of this somewhat infamous four-storey-high gatehouse derives from its position leading onto Micklegate, with the Old Norse *mykla gata* meaning 'great street'. Gate was Norwegian for 'street' and the numerous 'gates' in York and across much of Yorkshire bear testimony to their Viking origins. Connected to the 'great street' Micklegate Bar was traditionally the main ceremonial gate through which monarchs or other dignitaries entered York. A tradition established by Richard II in 1389 was for the monarch to touch the state sword as they passed through the gate. This route was used by every king of England from William the Conqueror to Henry VIII, with the exceptions of Richard the Lionheart and Edward V.

Micklegate Bar in the 1840s.

The twelfth-century gatehouse was rebuilt in the fourteenth century to gain a barbican with a heavy portcullis. The gateway became important as a symbol of power and traditionally the severed heads of traitors were displayed on spikes above the bar defences and there left to rot in public view. Famous heads paraded here included Henry (Harry) 'Hotspur' Percy (1403), Henry Scrope, 3rd Baron Scrope of Masham (1415), Richard Plantagenet, 3rd Duke of York (1460–61) displayed with a paper crown following the Battle of Wakefield, and Thomas Percy, 7th Earl of Northumberland (1572). There were many lesser victims too. With regard to Richard Plantagenet, Shakespeare famously wrote the following for Queen Margaret: 'off with his head and set it on York's gates; so York may overlook the Town of York.' Richard was removed in 1461 by King Edward IV following his victory at Towton; he was replaced by four Lancastrian heads. The final episode of heads on spikes here was after the Jacobite uprising in 1746, but they were stolen in 1754.

Fishergate Bar

Fishergate was built about 1315, and known as Barram Fishergate. The entrance was bricked up after rioting took place in 1489, and was only re-opened in the early nineteenth century.

Victoria Bar

The Victoria Bar was a very late addition, constructed in 1838, to give direct access to Nunnery Lane from Bishophill. During construction remains of a much older gateway

Fishergate Postern by A .G. Vickers, about 1835.

were discovered on the site. It is thought that this was perhaps a gateway known in the twelfth century as the *lounelith* or 'secluded gateway', by comparison to the 'great bar' at Micklegate. It may be that this was a minor entrance to York from the early medieval period when the walls were mostly a wooden palisade and prior to the medieval rebuilding in stone, but which was blocked with earth and rock.

Red Tower

As the names suggests, this structure is built of brick, constructed in 1490 after the uprising against King Henry VII. Even the construction of the Red Tower has a murky side because of a dispute between rival masons and tilers, the former resenting the latter winning the contract for the building work. As the arguments raged, with threats of mutilation, the masons smashed the tilers' tools, kilns and work. Finally they exacted their revenge when Master Tiler John Patrick was murdered by 'emasculation'. The masons, including William Hindley, the Master Mason of York Minster, were prosecuted but having taken sanctuary in York Minster precinct, were never convicted.

The tower was formerly considerably higher but its base is now under five feet of mud and silt after the nearby marsh was drained in the 1850s. The tower includes a projecting garderobe or toilet which emptied directly into the swamp below. The tiled roof is nineteenth century when the tower was restored for use as 'Brimstone House', a brimstone or gunpowder manufactory.

York Castle

Sadly, much of the once-great York castle has been removed and what remains gives just a hint of the earlier fortifications. The first castle, of Norman construction in 1068, was built for William I out of earth and wood. This structure was destroyed in the 1069 rebellion and rebuilt, again in wood. In 1190, the Clifford's Tower part of the castle was the site of the immolation of several hundred Jews, in part mass suicide and part massacre, by an anti-Jewish mob. This tower was rebuilt in wood, but during the period from 1245 to 1260 the castle, with Clifford's Tower, was reconstructed in stone for Henry III. The tower began to lean and crack quite early in its history, presumably the result of construction on the earthen mound. With rather mixed fortunes, the tower was severely burned in 1684 when a St George's Day Salute backfired. The castle in its later days became the debtors' prison and it was also here that the infamous highwayman Dick Turpin was held. In relation to its custodial function as a prison, from 1800 to 1868 public hangings were held in St George's Field outside the prison. After 1869 hangings became private affairs rather than public entertainment. York Castle was last used as a civilian prison in 1900 but continued as a military detention centre until 1929.

And Finally ...

The city has an almost unique time-line of military history and association. Furthermore, it has been connected to some of the finest military leaders and tacticians in history. It is interesting to look back over the lifespan of York and consider just a few of these in terms

Once the massive fortress, then the former Debtors' Prison, now York Castle Museum.

Clifford's Tower and the Castle walls pictured in the 1920s and giving a flavour of the former defences.

York from the city walls, pictured in the early 1900s.

of their significance to the place and in the history of warfare. With such a long military heritage this is a difficult task and the choice is subjective; some were great soldiers and others had a huge influence on the city.

First of all, the Roman generals must be considered because Quintus Cerialis, for example, established the fort that grew into the city. Agricola must rank as one of the great military leaders of all time and, but for his premature recall to Rome, would probably have brought almost all of Britain under imperial control. The records of others such as Hadrian don't bear close scrutiny, but that of Constantine the Great must place him above all in York's history. Declared Emperor of Rome while resident in York and the first Roman emperor to convert to Christianity, he stands as one of the great world leaders of all time. During the post-Roman period and early Saxon establishment we know relatively little of the military leaders. Indeed, the same can be said for some of the Viking period too. Nevertheless, Eric Bloodaxe is a name that many people still know and yet his life is shrouded in a large degree of mystery and no small amount of extreme violence. Even today, however, Eric is known as the last Viking king of York and an integral part of the story.

At about the same time, one of the greatest rulers of Dark Ages England, the Saxon King Athelstan, grandson of Alfred the Great, took York and united the kingdom at the cataclysmic Battle of Brunanburgh.

Other names from that time include Tostig Godwinson, but again this is more for his reputation for brutality than his skills as a military leader. If Harald Hardrada, king of Norway, had succeeded then he would certainly be one of York's greats, but he lost to Harold Godwinson. King Harold II is regarded as one of the finest military minds of his time; he persuaded his army to force-march from London to Stamford Bridge to defeat a Viking host and, furthermore, he led them back on foot via almost the same route to battle William at Hastings, testament not only to his military prowess but to his capacity as a leader. His victory at York was a Pyrrhic affair and yet he could easily have won at Hastings as well. As it is, history turns on such moments and York was at the core of the events and, indeed, it paid the price in its sacking and the subsequent 'Wasting of the North'.

William the Conqueror has to be included in our list, albeit with reluctance because of his genocidal treatment of the northern Saxons. Nevertheless, he instigated the building of York Castle and set in train the events which took York to prominence during the medieval period. Brutally cruel, it is also hard to dismiss the military achievements of William 'The Bastard', thus known because of his illegitimate birth. Richard Duke of York as King Richard II was a major figure of the time but sadly for him, his head ended up embellishing a Micklegate spike. However, his son King Edward IV won one of the most decisive battles on English soil and brought relative stability to a very troubled time. Richard III, despite the bad press from Shakespeare, has been reinvented in recent years as a sound administrator and an acknowledged brave and accomplished soldier. At Bosworth Field, he very nearly won the day by almost slaying Henry Tudor, but was cut down only yards from his objective.

Although the English Civil War is so called, the reality is that for much of the period after the Norman Conquest the country was at war to some degree or another. Certainly if we include the ongoing conflict with the Scots, then peaceful times were rare indeed. Of the Civil War leaders, there are several with close associations to York. However, the two outstanding military leaders were Oliver Cromwell on the Parliamentarian side and Prince Rupert for the Royalists. Though staunchly royalist, York proved to be Rupert's Waterloo and neither he nor the king's cause ever fully recovered from the defeat at Marston Moor. Lord Thomas Fairfax was one of the great Civil War leaders; he intervened to save the city from further damage by Roundhead looters.

The final name in York's military history comes in the Jacobite rebellions with Thomas Herring, Archbishop of York, described as 'the last warrior bishop of England'. The Duke of Cumberland was lauded by the city but major domestic conflict passed York by.

The military history of York has run a course of nearly 2,000 years, but in the early twenty-first century lives on only as heritage and the tourism economy. The city has grown alongside its political and strategic importance; it has waxed and waned with the fortunes, good and ill, of its kings, politicians and military leaders. Because of the strenuous efforts of those interested in York's historic features during the 1800s, a substantial part of the military heritage survives today and is now the cornerstone of one of the most successful and famous tourism attractions in the world.

SELECTED BIBLIOGRAPHY

Anon. (undated) *The Castle Museum York*. The Castle Museum York, York.

Anon. (undated) *Our Own Country. Descriptive, Historical, Pictorial*. Cassell, Petter, Galpin & Co., London.

Anon. (1978) *2000 Years of York – The Archaeological Story*. York Archaeological Trust, York.

Anon. (1972) *An Inventory of the Historical Monuments in the City of York, Volume II, The Defences*. Royal Commission on Historical Monuments, London.

Broadhead, I. E. (1989) *Yorkshire Battlefields. A Detailed Guide to 20 Historic Sites*. Robert Hale, London.

Burne, A .H. (1950) *The Battlefields of England*. Methuen, London.

Frere, S. (1967) *Britannia: A History of Roman Britain*. Routledge, London.

Hamilton, R. (2015) *Victoria Cross Heroes of World War One*. Atlantic, London.

Home, G. (1922) *York: A Sketch-Book*. A. & C. Black Ltd., London.

Home, G. (1936) *York Minster and Neighbouring Abbeys & Churches*. J. M. Dent & Sons Ltd., London.

Horton, R. W. (undated) *The City of York*. Pitkin Pictorials Ltd., London.

Mulhearn, K. (2002) *Fulford: The First Battle of 1066*. Roam'in Tours, York.

Oates, J. (2005) 'York and the Jacobite Rebellion of 1745'. *Borthwick Paper*, No. 107, Borthwick Institute, University of York, York.

Pallister, D. M. (2014) *Medieval York 600–1540*. Oxford University Press, Oxford.

Rayner, M. (2007) *English Battlefields*. Tempus, Stroud.

Rotherham, I. D. (2010) *Yorkshire's Forgotten Fenlands*. Pen & Sword Books Ltd., Barnsley.

Rotherham, I. D. (2015) *Lost York in Colour*. Amberley Publishing, Stroud.

Wellbeloved, C. (1842) *Eburacum or York under the Romans*. R. Sunter & H. Sotheran, York.

Willis, R. (undated) *York Castle Museum: The Living Past*. York Castle Museum, York.

Wilson, B. & Mee, F. (2009) *St Mary's Abbey and the King's Manor, York. The Pictorial Evidence*. The Archaeology of York Supplementary Series, Volume 1, York Archaeological Trust, York.

Wood, M. (1981) *In Search of the Dark Ages*. BBC Books, London.

ACKNOWLEDGEMENTS

I am most grateful to the historians and archaeologists who have done the essential primary research over many decades to unravel the stories of this fascinating city. However, I am equally indebted to the many unnamed enthusiasts who seek out and research, among others, old airfields and the remains of military heritage long since forgotten and neglected. Their sources and websites too numerous to mention are a rich mine of information that would otherwise be impossible to find.

ABOUT THE AUTHOR

Ian Rotherham discovered York Castle and walls on a childhood trip by steam train from Sheffield in the 1960s and has been going back ever since. He is Professor of Environmental Geography and Reader in Tourism & Environmental Change at Sheffield Hallam University, and as an ecologist and historian, he is a worldwide authority on landscape history, urban environments and environmental aspects of conflicts. He has researched and written about York and Yorkshire for many years, campaigning for their conservation, improvement and wider promotion. Having published over 500 papers, articles, books and book chapters, he has a popular BBC Radio Sheffield 'phone-in and writes for local and regional newspapers, particularly the *Sheffield Star*, the *Sheffield Telegraph*, and the *Yorkshire Post*. He is author of *Yorkshire's Forgotten Fenlands*

(Wharncliffe Publishing) and other books on York and Yorkshire. Ian lectures widely to local groups and works with bodies like The Wildlife Trusts, Natural England, Historic England, English Heritage, the National Trust and the RSPB. A Regional Tourism Ambassador for Sheffield and South Yorkshire, he works on major tourism and conservation projects across the county. He is a Fellow of the York-based PLACE (People, Landscape and the Cultural Environment) research centre.